# Protégé Profits

## How to Create a Legacy of Success Through Mentoring

Wayne Sharer

# Protégé Profits

Copyright © 2012 Wayne Sharer
www.waynesharer.com

ISBN-13:978-1479350384

ISBN-10:1479350389

**All Rights Reserved. No part of this publication may be reproduced in any form or by any means, including scanning, photocopying, or otherwise without prior written permission of the copyright holder.**

Disclaimer and Terms of Use: The Author and Publisher has strived to be as accurate and complete as possible in the creation of this book, notwithstanding the fact that she does not warrant or represent at any time that the contents within are accurate due to the rapidly changing nature of the Internet. While all attempts have been made to verify information provided in this publication, the Author and Publisher assumes no responsibility for errors, omissions, or contrary interpretation of the subject matter herein. Any perceived slights of specific persons, peoples, or organizations are unintentional. In practical advice books, like anything else in life, there are no guarantees of income made. Readers are cautioned to rely on their own judgment about their individual circumstances to act accordingly. This book is not intended for use as a source of legal, business, accounting or financial advice. All readers are advised to seek services of competent professionals in the legal, business, accounting, and finance fields.

# DEDICATION

To all those who have fallen in service, your lives make a difference.  To all my mentors, for making it possible for me to never quit and make a radical difference in others' lives, no matter what.  To Leslie for believing.

# Protégé Profits

# Table of Contents

Welcome to Protégé Profits..................................................7

*Chapter 1* ............................................................................. 13
   The Advantages of Having a Protégé

*Chapter 2* ............................................................................. 23
   What You Give Your Protégé in Return

*Chapter 3* ............................................................................. 29
   Where Are All The Protégés Hiding?

*Chapter 4* ............................................................................. 39
   Now That You Found Your Protégé, What's Next?

*Chapter 5* ............................................................................. 53
   Keeping The Communication Lines Open

*Chapter 6* ............................................................................. 77
   Working Side By Side

*Chapter 7* ............................................................................. 95
   Time To Call It A Night

*Chapter 8* ............................................................................ 101
   A Squadron of Protégés

*Chapter 9* ............................................................................ 107
   Repeating The Process

Final Thoughts .................................................................. 111

Appendix ........................................................................... 115
   How To Be A Professional Altruist

About The Author ............................................................. 111

# Protégé Profits

# Welcome to Protégé Profits

## The Mentor-Protégé Relationship

Welcome to a long term gold mine of insights and techniques on how to do something totally enjoyable, completely fulfilling, and highly valuable in both relationships and business profits. If you're like me, you like having people you know understand what you want and carry out your mission almost as if they were you. You may even be thinking, "Yeah that's great, what a dreamer."

I agree with you that this could just be a dream for most and I'll add this is very possible, and very enjoyable, and also much easier than you think, if you're mind is open to growth.
I completely understand that you want in your business activity that is truly profitable. At the same time, you would like it if some of your most profitable activities happened to be fun. Fun is good for everyone, am I right?

That's the cool thing about mentoring. Unlike making to-do lists, having meetings, conducting strategy sessions, or planning next year's budget, mentoring a protégé not only is fun and rewarding for both you and your protégé, it's also profitable over an extremely long term.

## What is Mentoring?

There are few experiences more rewarding than teaching what you know to someone else, and then your student taking that knowledge and succeeding with it. The mentor-protégé relationship is perhaps the ultimate teaching experience: a one-on-one transfer of accumulated knowledge and wisdom designed to benefit you and your student. Often your protégé ends up (in a sense) becoming you, and carrying your efforts as if he or she can read your mind.

Protégés are a common occurrence in the business world today. Experienced people in every industry often decide to "adopt" a protégé—whether the arrangement is through a formal mentoring program, or an informal mutual decision to take a new employee "under your wing" and show him the ropes. The reasons to enter into a mentor-protégé relationship are many, but the most common is when the protégé candidate shows promise from the start.

I used mentoring-protégé relationships throughout my military career, though generally in an informal way; mostly in an unconscious way.

I realized mentor-protégé relationships can be either formal or informal. Informal mentoring relationships often develop on their own, with the more experienced person offering advice and assistance, and the newcomer taking that advice to heart. This is pretty much what happened with me in my Navy career. However, many organizations have formal mentoring programs, which can be either within the company or within the industry. For example, the Small Business Administration runs a mentoring program where retired business executives dedicate their time to developing protégés. I'm not endorsing this program, just mentioning it as an example familiar to many of you.

College interns also figure into the equation. Though protégés are not always interns, the relationships are virtually the same, while the reasoning may be different. Do you remember your days in college? Remember the many professor assistants who may have taught you many classes? But whether you work with a protégé or a college intern, becoming a mentor can be one of the most rewarding experiences of your professional life because it can bring profits to your business, and create massive success for others.

**A Brief History of Mentoring**

The actual origins of the mentoring process are unknown. However, the word "mentor" is derived from Homer's Odyssey. The original "Mentor" was an older man who served as an advisor to the king. Unfortunately, Mentor was rather ineffectual in his advice. However, the term in this context refers to the goddess Athena, who took on the form of Mentor to advise a younger man in the art of war.

There have been many famous mentor-protégé pairs throughout history. One of the earliest and most well-known was Paul of Tarsus and Timothy, a first-century Christian bishop. Minister, activist, and Morehouse college president Dr. Benjamin Elijah Mays served as a mentor to Martin Luther King, Jr.; and the poet Ezra Pound guided a fledgling T.S. Eliot through his literary career.

Most recently, the protégé concept has been illustrated through billionaire Donald Trump's reality television show, The Apprentice, where young men and women compete for the opportunity to claim Trump as their business mentor. This is an extreme level of publicity, but you get the point. Learning a trade or an industry from someone with more experience has been a consistent occurrence throughout history, and it is still a viable and successful approach.

# Protégé Profits

This book explains how to find and develop a protégé in the modern business world. You will discover the benefits to you and your business and the benefits of taking on a protégé; where to look for one, how to cultivate a relationship, and how to know when it's time for your protégé to spread his wings and fly solo.

You don't have to be Ezra Pound or Donald Trump to offer something worthwhile to a protégé. If you've had experience in a business or industry, you can benefit from adding someone new to your field and have the pleasure of watching new talent unfold. If your passions are shared by many, then you know more than someone else, and you can grow your apprentice. Doing so will help your company profit, and build wildly successful futures for others.

**How Having and Being a Mentor Impacted Me**

Before you dive in, think back in your own life. What impact did a mentor have on you? I know for me, even though it was informal, the relationship determined the way I thought about myself.

My first tour of duty in a real Navy carrier-based squadron determined my future. Though the associations weren't thought of as mentor-protégé relationships, my first real mentor was the commanding officer of that squadron.

We were returning from a very long deployment on the USS America. We stopped in Signolla, Sicily, an island off Italy, and one evening there in the "Fly Trap" officer's bar he said to me after a few beers, "Wayne, you are going to be a C.O. (commanding officer) one day. "

# Protégé Profits

He then handed me his leather flight jacket to wear. I was in awe. And those words stuck with me the rest of my time in the Navy. I did become exactly what he said. The power of the mentor is, in many ways, unimaginable.

The rest of my 22 years as a Naval Flight Officer I saw myself as a leader and mentor. It was, of course, very important to me to succeed, for failure in the Navy while flying over 200 combat missions from aircraft carriers could easily mean death. The reality of death made it vital that I have protégés who could replace me, and do what I do as good, or better than me. It made our unit (business) run smoother, made us more productive, and ensured I got some personal time to do things I wanted or needed to do for me.

The only difference in a private business is your decisions or failures won't likely cause death. This doesn't change the need to breed creativity, resourcefulness, and passing on the ability to add value when you are not around. Your personal freedom and prosperity depend on you, and how well you choose your protégé.

Now let's dig in, and discover what mentoring can do for your business and profits, as well as what it does for your charge.

> *"And in the end it is not the years in your life that count, it's the life in your years."*
> ~Abraham Lincoln~

# Protégé Profits

# Chapter 1
## The Advantages of Having a Protégé

**It's a Two-Way Street**

The advantages to having a mentor are beneficial, and most people understand that. But none the less, there are quite a few rewards mentors receive from participating in the process—some more apparent than others. You'll learn more about this here.

What's really behind your desire in becoming a mentor? Perhaps you work for a company with a mentoring program, and you feel ready to lend your expertise. Or maybe you've noticed someone who has that same spark of motivation and drive you possessed when you first entered your career, or started you business. Whatever your reason, you will find that mentoring gives as much as it takes. This is the part many business people miss.

Here are just a few of the benefits you will receive by taking on a protégé.

**A fresh outlook**

No matter who you choose to work with, your protégé will have a different perspective on the business. Don't look for someone who only thinks the way you do. Since protégés are typically entry-level professionals (though not necessarily), they will possess new ideas and new ways of thinking that you may not have been aware of before. Their perspective and vision may be completely different from yours. If you look for your clone, you will likely never find your protégé.

# Protégé Profits

Mentors definitely do learn as much from protégés as their charges learn from them. One of the most recent examples of this can be found in the impact that the Internet has had on the business world. When companies began to rely on e-mail communication and drift away from phones and fax machines, those who possessed the greatest knowledge of e-communication were the entry-level staff; the ones who had recently graduated from college or grew up with the Internet. It's a safe bet that today's protégés are able to show their mentors a thing or two about online procedures!

Don't mistake this with who invented the mediums. The so-called "baby boomers" invented this. Yet those exposed to it as a part of life embrace it much faster.

The enthusiasm a protégé brings to the relationship through this embracing of fresh ideas is another factor in offering a fresh outlook. Today's business is competitive and draining for most people. It is easy to lose your passion for your career or your business after you've been at it for years. Working with a protégé allows you to revisit the ideals and visions that brought you to work in your field in the first place.

In fact, you most likely will increase your creativity and, if you're a business owner, find the inspiration for new products.

**Personal satisfaction**

Becoming a mentor is immensely satisfying on a personal level. You have the opportunity to make a difference in another person's life, and help them step up to the often-difficult realm of business success with confidence. You will be giving your protégé the gift of knowledge that they cannot find in books or classes.

Witnessing and taking part in the developmental process of tomorrow's leaders is a phenomenal experience. Imagine the pride Benjamin Mays must have felt as Martin Luther King, Jr., made such great strides in the civil rights movement. In effect, Mays was just as influential in changing the face of America as King himself. This is the true power of mentoring. In my navy days, and now personal business, watching people take what I give them and turn it into massive success creates an inner feeling of immense satisfaction not matched by anything else I do. Often, the protégé never realized how truly satisfying working with them was for me.

By working with a protégé, you can create a living archive of knowledge and experience that will be passed on through generations. Those who have benefited from you as a mentor are likely to become mentors themselves and attempt to give back what they have received. The mentor-protégé relationship represents a never-ending cycle of information to which anyone can contribute.

**Sharper skills**

As a mentor, you may already be in a management, leadership, or business owner position—and you may not. Regardless of your current career designation, working with a protégé will help you develop those skills essential to leading others, which could in turn lead you to a promotion, new business ideas, or more profits for your business.

# Protégé Profits

It's also very possible, if not likely, you won't be in direct charge of your protégé. However, the process of mentoring involves guidance and correction. It's being that very special coach. You will be responsible for overseeing your protégé's skill development; in essence, "showing the ropes."

Communication is an essential tool for any business and leadership relationship. By working with a protégé, you will find your communication skills developing almost automatically, and exponentially. Mentoring is a journey of self-discovery, as well as a means to help a highly motivated person get a great start in the business world for career purposes, or for starting their own business.

My love of commanding a navy aviation squadron was driven by the ability to shape younger officers for the prospect of "taking my place" and doing even better than me.

I can remember the looks from my young department heads when they seemed amazed I knew things about their people and the aircraft, and they really couldn't figure out how I knew them. I would drop them tips and tricks through suggestions. I would wonder around listening, and then pass on what I found in department head meetings. This would drive them to find out more before I could find out, which in reality was much easier for them to do then for me.

## Career development

As you further your protégé's career, you are advancing your own as well. As mentioned previously, working with a protégé within your company can present the opportunity for promotion. Your supervisors will take note of your progress during the relationship.

# Protégé Profits

You can also apply the skills you develop in grooming your protégé to other areas of your job. This will allow you to implement changes and new projects that will help you stand out and get noticed. Should you decide to change careers or companies, including your mentoring work on your resume can be a huge plus—particularly if your protégé is successful.

**Free labor**

This may seem a little shallow, but protégés can and do perform routine tasks and help with project research and development. They are also willing to share ideas which will dramatically change your results as the mentor. This is not taking advantage of your young charge; rather, it is allowing them to be a part of the process from the beginning. It is far more effective to learn a trade through doing rather than watching, and assigning small tasks to your protégé helps both of you.

I remember well how my dad used to teach me. He never let me touch anything. He made me watch and absorb. After watching, and evaluating, I was expected to copy the task on my own. The part where I really grasped the effort was when I did the task for real. He taught me skills in auto repair, carpentry, plumbing, and much more this way. He was an amazing mentor without ever realizing it, and he got a lot of work done that he may never have completed on his own.

**Higher self-image**

*"Leadership is solving problems. The day soldiers stop bringing you their problems is the day you have stopped leading them. They have either lost confidence that you can help or have*

# Protégé Profits

*concluded you do not care. Either case is a failure of leadership".*
~Colin Powell~

The way you view yourself reflects in the way others view you. When you work with a protégé, you will build your self-esteem as you realize how much you have to offer a young person in your business. Often, mentors find they had no idea how much they really knew about their industry or passions until they began to teach it to someone else.

This elevated self-image for you as a mentor will in turn change the way your colleagues and supervisors view you. Mentors are respected for their dedication and willingness to help others flourish. You will command greater respect and a higher level of prestige when you work with a protégé. Others will see you as a person of great value.

Mentors enjoy a strong sense of confidence in their knowledge and their abilities to lead. Success comes easier when you feel good about what you're doing, and your success is totally dependent on your perception of yourself.

**Mentoring: Do you have what it takes?**

How do you know when you're ready to take on a protégé? Effective mentors possess particular qualities that will assist them in taking another person through the steps of developing a successful career.

The following skill sets are important for any mentor to develop:

# Protégé Profits

## Communication and rapport

Mentoring is basically an exchange of information. You must be able to not only effectively communicate your ideas, but also be able to constructively interpret your protégé's goals and activities. It is good to possess knowledge, but hard to pass that knowledge on if you can't present it within a framework others can understand.

Your ability to put things into multiple frameworks will truly enhance your mentoring abilities. If you are the kind of person who really doesn't like to see things in different ways, then you probably won't find mentoring very satisfying.

Getting along with your protégé is also an important consideration. If you're not the type that "plays well with others," entering a mentor-protégé relationship will be a challenge for you. It is difficult for two people who don't like each other to work together. Rapport-building skills allow you to establish a common ground and let both parties remain at ease during the mentoring process.

> *"The way we communicate with others and with ourselves ultimately determines the quality of our lives".*
> ~Anthony Robbins~

## Insider information

A good mentor will offer a protégé more than he or she would be able to gain from traditional routes, such as college courses and self-help books. Sorry, college professors, but there is no better instruction in life than reality.

# Protégé Profits

I remember when I was in college, how so many of the professors had this air of self-appointed importance. So much so, they considered your learning being something done on their time, so you owed them to listen outright, without challenge, to whatever they said.

Having a strong, real-world knowledge of industry protocol can give you an edge in the mentor process. This generally is lacking in the classroom. As someone who has "been there, done that", you have a better perspective on what works and what doesn't in real-world applications of your industry's established protocol.

It is also beneficial to be familiar with methods for getting ahead. Career advancement is a rather fluid process in most business areas, with no real set of rules governing the procedures. Promotions are rarely a simple matter of working hard and doing your best. Often, networking and keeping up with current trends can mean the difference between stagnation and advancement. Your ability to network and pass this on in a skillful way to your protégé helps you learn the difference between developing valuable relationships and just simply kissing ass.

Another much-lauded buzzword in today's business world is diversity. As a mentor, you should be familiar with the diversity issues that affect your industry, on both demographic and skill levels. This presents further opportunity to educate your protégé in the actual practices of your career area.

# Protégé Profits

You, as a mentor, can show a clear value to diversity in a real, value added sense, versus the political liberal sense of forced diversity, which has proven to have no value in real life.

## Experience and balance

It goes without saying that an effective mentor will have experience. However, you may not be aware that one of the most important areas to have experience in is loving your job. If you lack passion for what you're doing, you cannot expect to inspire a newcomer to succeed. At the least, you should have passion for what your career should accomplish in a perfect world—even if the reality has shown you otherwise. Working with a protégé can present another opportunity to make a difference in your industry.

Balance is essential for any successful career. As a mentor, you are likely to have already learned how to balance work and family so that neither area suffers from lack of attention. Because you are familiar with the actual demands of your industry, you can help your protégé find that balance in his own life.

## Honesty and integrity

Despite the media generated idea that corruption is not only widespread and that it's almost expected in the working world today, honesty is still the best policy, and is what is at the heart of all highly successful businesses. Those who have risen to their positions through actual success make far better mentors than those who were less than straightforward with their dealings (can you say Enron?). Dishonest mentors create dishonest protégés, and ultimately failure—and that's not good for anyone.

Integrity is another important qualification for mentors. Historically significant change in any industry has come about only through those who refuse to compromise their ideals. The best mentors possess strong personal morals and the ability to resist taking the easy way when it would mean diminishing their integrity.

If you are confident in your position, you are in a good place to work with a protégé. It is difficult to impart stability and growth if you live in fear of downsizing or corporate manipulation. In a successful and flourishing industry, there is always room for new talent—and as a mentor, you get to play a strategic role in introducing new talent to your business community.

**Organization**

It is nearly impossible to succeed in business without an organized approach. Most mentors are on their way to mastering organizational skills or have mastered them; an area that can prove one of the most challenging to newcomers. Your protégé will learn how to get things done with your guidance, whether you are teaching them how to keep paperwork straight, coordinate a massive sales force, or build their own business.

If you don't see yourself in every aspect of this list, take heart: the mentoring process will allow you to develop those areas in which you may not have the greatest strengths. Remember, the mentor-protégé relationship works to benefit both of you. You will learn what you don't already know along the way.

# Chapter 2
## What You Give Your Protégé In Return

Protégés also tend to benefit greatly from the mentoring experience. As with the benefits to the mentor, there are the obvious and the not-so-obvious advantages. It is a good idea to be familiar with the benefits to a protégé, as it will help you define the relationship and determine the best areas to concentrate on during the process.

What will your protégé receive from you? I can't begin to detail everything you or your protégé gain. This chapter covers just a few of the rewarding benefits of you providing mentoring.

### Knowledge

This, of course, is the most apparent and tangible benefit to a protégé. The mentoring process presents the opportunity to gain wisdom with real applications in the business world. In every industry and in the transition from high school or college, there is a discernible gap between training and practice. Mentors can help protégés smooth that gap and avoid much of the trial-and-error process that plagues most career paths.

### Challenge

Mentoring presents an unparalleled opportunity for challenge in any industry, and the best protégés challenge themselves to excel. Protégés strive to live up to the expectations and achievements of their mentors, or even surpass them. This, in turn, provides a challenge to the mentor, further enriching the experience.

# Protégé Profits

As a mentor, you must present a challenge to your protégé or you are cheating him or her, or not even realizing a potential they could never have imagined themselves. Mentors don't tell their protégés they did everything great. A true mentor presents a challenge, and criticizes the results starting with something good, detailing the bad very directly, and then finishing with something good – a road to success, so to speak.  Don't be a coward mentor.

*"Any fool can criticize, condemn and complain – and most do."*
~Dale Carnegie~

**Improved self-confidence**

When you agree to be a mentor consciously or subconsciously, you are asserting your belief that the protégé is worth your time and effort. This in turn allows the protégé to feel confident in his or her abilities and talents. Genuine praise is a rare commodity in business, and the acceptance of a mentor-protégé relationship is a great confidence booster for both parties. The mentor is honored that someone wants to learn from them, and the protégé is pleased that someone feels they have potential.

A good mentor also offers support and reassurance to a protégé. Mistakes are met with suggestions to improve rather than threats against employment. Often simply knowing that support is available proves enough to allow protégés to flourish, as they don't have to fear going it alone.

Little tricks of the so-called old school mentors like Dale Carnegie remain as true today as they ever were "back in the day."  If you haven't read "How to Win Friends and Influence

# Protégé Profits

People," you should. The point is, using his "trick" of letting your protégé believe they came up with new ideas through suggestion creates a level of results and potential profits from your charge you likely never imagined.

## A straighter path to success

The road to success in any industry is paved with peril and pitfalls. For a protégé, teaming with a mentor can mean the opportunity to bypass some of the side roads and stay focused on success.

Of course, this also translates to faster financial gain for you, your protégé and (if you're a business owner) your business. It often takes years to build measurable success, and mentors allow this process to unfold faster. There are not many who would say no to earlier raises and promotions, or faster growth of your personal business!

## New opportunities

For a protégé, obtaining a mentor is a chance to explore areas that may not be open to their colleagues. The mentor-protégé relationship lends new meaning to the phrase "getting in on the ground floor." Mentors can help to define a career path, particularly in sprawling industries with many directions in which a young person can move. A protégé is allowed a look at the specific avenues to success for a given department or function.

As a mentor, or accepting your place as a mentor, you pass on a real feeling of belonging to your protégé. Without this relationship, the "new guy" is left to flounder, and their productivity is much slower developed (read this as delayed profit potential!)

## A non-threatening learning experience

Corporate culture often comes as a shock to those just entering the workforce. Actually, this is an understatement. It always comes as a shock to new entries. The pressure to compete and succeed emanates from all sides, and it is easy to flounder in the face of such pressure.

Protégés enjoy a certain protection from the strain of competition. They are allowed to learn and develop under the guidance of an experienced mentor, and assured of their place in the industry. The measure of job security a protégé receives is definitely a powerful motivator to strive for the best and make a positive impact in the world.

I dare say, if in my early years in the Navy as a struggling junior officer, if someone like my first commanding officer had never offered any indication of where they saw me, my career would have been significantly different.

How can I say this? Even though I did not live the life without the direction occurring, I know that throughout my career, his boldly and confidently telling me I would be a commanding officer registered in my thoughts the entire time.

## Long term relationships and networking opportunities

When it comes to business, it is often not so much what you know as who you know. This is not to say that those who are

# Protégé Profits

inept can advance by virtue of their connections (though, unfortunately, this does happen). Remember, there is a limit to this type of inept advancement. Eventually, it catches up with the recipient.

However, a talented protégé can achieve recognition faster and be introduced to those who might actually be able to influence their careers. The mentor is the key, and makes it happen without all the corporate "ass kissing" that occurs in the lower and mid-levels. Flattery and agreement are certainly pleasant, but they don't bring profits, and they don't help your protégé realize their full abilities.

The relationship forged between mentor and protégé can be a long lasting affair that will continue to benefit both parties. Even when the process of knowledge transference ends, mentors often become colleagues, partners, or simply good and supportive friends.

Your power to literally determine the future of your protégé is likely something you won't realize until you embrace the value. Watch your charge grow. Implant ideas in their head. Create the challenges, and watch how you, your business and your protégé all profit in many ways from the experience.

Protégé Profits

# Chapter 3
## Where Are The Protégés Hiding?

As previously mentioned, mentor programs can be formal or informal, and the structure varies according to the participants and the way in which the partnership comes about. So if you've finally decided you would like to work with a protégé, there are several places you can look for one.

**Your company**

Whether or not your company, or you as the owner of your business, has a formal mentor program, a great place to find a protégé is right in front of you. Informally, the procedure is simple: find someone you work with who shows promise and may be struggling, and offer to help them succeed. If the person you ask truly wants to learn and advance, they will not refuse.

Promise is usually seen in the form of the prospective protégé showing great motivation in the form of self-action. The power protégé is one who can look at things, analyze them, and take action without direction. Those who consistently wait for permission for everything really don't possess what you want – unless you cause the permission-based atmosphere. If this is the case, then you as the mentor will have to open up, or you won't likely ever find the person you're looking for.

Today, many companies recognize the potential success of mentoring programs and will have a formal structure in place. In this situation, you would offer your services as a mentor to the coordinator of your company's program, and would then be matched to a protégé. Depending on your company's procedures, the matching process may entail:

- Potential mentors requesting a specific employee to work with
- Pairing based on questionnaires, employment records, or job details
- The coordinator assigning mentors to those who request them
- Match-ups based on mutual consent
- Or a combination of these procedures

Formal mentor programs can be quite successful when they are well structured. One of the benefits of a formal mentor program is that it will often include advancement for both parties based on monitored performance. Volunteering to become a mentor creates a favorable image; if done well, it can lead to greater recognition within your company.

If your company does not have a formal mentor program, you may want to consider proposing or creating one yourself. A good mentor program takes into account the needs and restrictions of the mentor, the protégé candidate, and the company as a whole. Any organization in any industry can benefit from a mentor program on many levels.

I have to caution you though. Sometimes formal programs work on the idea that anyone can be a protégé, and anyone can be a mentor. This definitely is not true. Even in formal programs, the mentor must be a skilled guide, and not dictator, and the protégé must have real desire and motivation to achieve personal success, and success in the business mission.

# Protégé Profits

## Mentoring programs

Many professional organizations maintain mentor matching services, and most of them are free for both mentors and protégés. With a mentor matching service, you can benefit through a screening process that improves the chances of the relationship succeeding.

Perhaps you aren't looking for a business protégé, and simply want to help a young person succeed. Two of the largest mentoring programs in the country are geared for general life experience mentoring, and offer mentors a rich opportunity to change the life of another person:

### *Big Brothers Big Sisters*

The Big Brothers Big Sisters (BBBS) program is the largest mentoring program in the country. This organization is dedicated to improving the lives of underprivileged children by pairing them with an adult volunteer mentor and developing a relationship.

Big Brothers and Big Sisters typically meet with their partners, or "Littles," two to four times a month. Participating in BBBS can be challenging, as many of the children have difficulties trusting adults; however, it is also one of the most rewarding experiences available.

You can learn more about BBBS on their website at www.bbbsa.org.

### *SCORE*

The Service Corps of Retired Executives Association (SCORE) is dedicated to counseling entrepreneurs and professionals in their chosen careers. You don't have to be retired to volunteer as a mentor through SCORE; they currently have a network of over 10,000 volunteers donating their knowledge and skills to individuals across the country.

SCORE matches professionals with protégés on a face-to-face basis as well as virtually. As a mentor, you have the option of working remotely or arranging personal counseling sessions through one of the organization's 389 offices.

To sign up as a mentor with SCORE, visit www.score.org.

**College Interns**

College interns are not quite the same as protégés, but they serve many of the same functions and can be just as beneficial to work with. If you decide to hire a college intern, you may create a temporary low-paying position, or you might get an intern to work for free.

The main difference between interns and protégés is that protégés are seeking the benefit of a mentor's knowledge to advance careers they have already begun, while interns are simply looking for the experience that will allow them to land a good position when they graduate. This translates to a difference in attitudes and expectations: while a protégé works with you to learn, an intern is there to do.

Interns typically are eager to prove their value, and they expect to perform many of your tasks for you, where a protégé may simply be content to "watch and learn." A possible disadvantage is interns are available only when they are not attending classes, and you may end up having to pay a small salary, as many college students can no longer afford to work for free.

Where do you find a college intern? Generally, you find them through a local college, university counselor's office, or community relations. This will vary from school to school. You can usually go directly to the college's guidance or employment center to advertise for an intern. If there are several colleges in your area, you might consider placing a newspaper ad to announce the availability of the internship you're offering.

Whether you go through a college or a classified ad, it is important to specify what you are looking for in an intern, and what the internship will entail. Your listing should include:

- Detailed job description, including expected duties, number of days and hours to be worked, and rate of pay if applicable
- The desired type of college major
- Best way to contact you (phone, fax, e-mail) and what to send (message, resume, referrals, transcripts)
- Your company name
- Your company address
- Your name and position
- Contact telephone number
- E-mail address
- Fax number

You should run your advertisement for at least two weeks, and then begin the interviewing process. Just as in a job interview, be sure to ask both open-ended and closed-ended questions. When interviewing interns, look for the qualities detailed in the following chapter on picking a protégé.

Working with a college intern can be a satisfying experience, and provide many of the same benefits to both parties as a mentor-protégé relationship.

**Other companies or industry segments**

Cross-company mentoring can also be successful, provided it does not occur between two competing companies. Some industries are more conducive to this type of mentoring than others; for example, if you work at Pepsi, you would not want to choose a protégé employed by Coca Cola. However, if you are a consultant or work in an industry that must be "broken into," such as publishing, there is no shortage of up-and-comers who will value your advice.

However, this doesn't mean there is some specific company type where it's best. Any companies, in any industry can have these exchanges if they operate with some high level of trust. Think about this: don't you think that Pepsi already has people who worked at Coca Cola in ranks and vice versa? Now, this is just an example made up off the top of my head. I have no inside knowledge of Pepsi and Coca Cola's business relationships.

One way to find a protégé outside your company is through word of mouth. It sounds simple, but many people would not think of this. You can simply let your industry contacts know that you are looking to take on a protégé, and ask them to tell you if they learn of someone who might be a match. This brings the added benefit of making the protégé a lot more confident when they are approached first, rather than having them come to you.

You can also look to the Internet to find a protégé. There are online communities in every industry where like minds gather to chat and you may find just what you're looking for in an online network. There are forums and blogs, and advertising spots in virtually any profitable industry waiting for you online.

Long distance mentor-protégé relationships are a viable alternative with the ready availability of electronic communication, so you could have a protégé who is halfway across the country and still maintain an effective relationship. This will take a little more skill, but if you have any experience in virtual business, or working in industries where much of your business is long-distance or international, then you would be well suited for this.

## Happenstance

This is a surprisingly common scenario in the business world. It's certainly how the relationships developed in the Navy for me. I didn't understand how things were happening; they just sort of did, mostly because of the results produced. Thus it's very common for a relationship between a mentor and a protégé to develop on its own.

It may happen when an experienced professional will take notice of someone new to the company or industry scene and offer advice, or a young person will ask an insightful question of a seasoned pro. If the initial exchange establishes a connection or a common interest, the communication tends to naturally continue. Eventually they are connecting on a regular basis, and have become an informal mentor-protégé pair.

This was very common for me, particularly as a squadron commanding officer. My duty was to find my replacements. Those that engaged me in leadership this way, with real concerns, real ideas, and real understanding of their mission were my informal protégé targets. When I found them, I made a personal, yet covert choice to "feed" these new charges with "rudder commands" designed to steer them. If they could take the hint and develop it, I knew I had the right person.

Many times a chance connection can spark the strongest mentoring relationships. Prime examples of this are those that occur in creative industries like books or film and television. Many aspiring actors and writers have gotten their "big breaks" by interacting with established successes in the industry. In fact, writers and actors are encouraged to seek out mentors to improve their chances in what can be extremely difficult fields to break into.

There is also a downside to this method. It can occur in any mentor-protégé relationship, but most often happens in those begun by chance. Sometimes, a mentor will wrongly evaluate the potential of a young person, and by the time the error becomes apparent may insist on continuing to recommend their protégé in order to save face. It is difficult to admit mistakes, particularly when it comes to protégés. Avoiding this scenario will be further discussed in the following chapter of this book.

# Chapter 4
## Now That You Found Your Protégé, What's Next?

*"I'm a success today because I had a friend who believed in me and I didn't have the heart to let him down."*
~ Abraham Lincoln~

Ok. You've decided to take on a protégé. You're going to have to be selective about who you're going to work with. This is important on so many several levels. You don't want to end up training someone you will not be able to recommend to others, so for both you and your protégé, it must be worth the time you will spend mentoring.

As a mentor, you will be doing your protégé a favor by helping them succeed; but keep in mind that they're also doing you a favor by providing you with experience, knowledge, and a new perspective on your industry. When you choose smartly for both you and your charge, the return to you will be both rewarding personally, and profitable. Neither you nor your protégé should feel superior to one another; mentoring is a process of give and take.

In this chapter, we'll discuss how to select a protégé that best matches you and your goals, and how to avoid making poor choices.

**Ingredients of a good protégé**

Not all business executives and professionals make good mentors, and not every newcomer will flourish as a protégé. But a successful protégé will possess certain qualities.

# Protégé Profits

Here are some of the qualities you should keep in mind when selecting a protégé. Some are more easily identifiable than others, but nonetheless, important.

## Receptive and open to new ideas and new ways of learning

An open mind is an essential key to business success. There are always new ideas, techniques, and methods that prove surprisingly effective. When picking a protégé, be sure your candidate is willing to consider possibilities outside the realm of his experience—and remember to keep an open mind yourself.

Look out for people who say things like, "this is the way I always do it," or flatly respond to new ideas with replies such as, "that can't possibly work." This is a bad sign in a new protégé. It's also a bad sign for you as a mentor if these are replies *you* commonly use and they stop you from thinking things through.

I used to have a quick response to things striking me as not making sense before I thought them out. I used say, "that's stupid," or "don't be stupid."

Though I was completely aware of this, and it didn't stop me from going and thinking things out afterwards, my junior officers were also keenly aware of this. When an aviation commanding officer is leaving the squadron, the junior officers traditionally do a skit to make fun of the departing C.O., and naturally they pick on the things that most annoyed them. For me, they kept making fun of my over use of the word "stupid."

# Protégé Profits

*"We are all born ignorant, but one must work hard to remain stupid."*
~Benjamin Franklin~

## Good communication and cooperative work skills

Just as you must be able to articulate your ideas, so must your protégé. Choose to work with someone who can communicate effectively, who expresses his or her qualifications and intentions clearly from the start. If you cannot understand what the candidate wants from the relationship, you cannot expect to meet goals on either end.

Whatever your native business language is, your protégé must be capable of communicating clearly. If your prospective protégé wants to talk to clients in colloquialisms not used in business, and can't be corrected, then you must move on in your selection.

Young individuals who think everything is about their personal identity don't really understand business, and will cause you to lose both esteem, and money. I don't advocate everyone is the same, but your business has a mission, and your protégé must be able to communicate it. Your business is about your customers and giving them value, not about employees trying to maintain selfish identities.

So you also must be able to work together with your protégé. Beware of those who are too driven, or who seem intent on asserting their own merits. Often, the ego-centric protégé will have already developed a sense of superiority that makes them difficult to work with, no matter how talented they might be. Drive is necessary—but so is a certain degree of humility.

# Protégé Profits

This sort of "chip on the shoulder" is usually very evident. Sometimes, the arrogance will be more disguised. It will manifest itself in protégés gestures, and the facial expressions they use when communicating with you. These are subtle but obvious, and should be challenged by you.

**A strong sense of personal responsibility**

Whether they are good or bad, a successful businessperson takes responsibility for his own actions. Be sure your protégé is able to accept responsibility and refrain from passing blame onto circumstances or other people.

It is all too common to encounter overdeveloped senses of entitlement. Since the days of the hippie culture in the US, thriving groups of people have succumb to the idea that those doing the work have to give what they make to them, and it's not their fault they do nothing.

Strive to work with a protégé who is self-aware and does not institutionalize or redirect blame. Unfortunately, a lack of personal responsibility can lead to legal complications and public spectacle.

The only chance of creating a true success is for your protégé to fully accept accountability for his or her actions, and not blame others constantly. Sure, there are times when other people will prevent you from reaching your goal initially. But it's your fault if you keep dealing with them, and don't redirect your efforts elsewhere.

You know this as a business person. You know you must provide value to your customers, and you must profit. You also know you have choices and every choice you make has an effect on you and your business. Your protégé must be willing to embrace this so you can really develop the relationship successfully, and your business continues to prosper.

**A commitment to expanding skills and capabilities**

Good protégés are committed to themselves and their career, will always be grateful for your guidance, and want to learn. This must be part of their nature, and not something you can give them. You do not want to work with someone who is content to merely report for work and bring home a paycheck each week. Try to select a protégé who displays genuine interest in the workings of your industry, and is truly excited about the prospect of a successful long-term career.

This is truly self-motivation. They need to be someone who takes action independently, even at risk of being wrong. Your protégé must be motivated without the fear failure being an inhibitor. Everyone fears failure, but the real future builders don't let this stop them.

**The ability to accept and act upon constructive criticism**

Accepting criticism objectively is a difficult skill to master; applying it even more so. Your protégé should possess the ability to listen to criticism without taking it personally, and the necessary detachment to use comments constructively. No one wants to work with a prima donna. It will strain the relationship if you end up having to carefully monitor what you have to say in order to avoid hurt feelings.

# Protégé Profits

This isn't to be mistaken to mean that criticism won't have the initial effect of hurting your charges feelings. This is the real world, and of course the criticism causes an initial negative feeling in anyone. What you look for is a protégé who can absorb it, and turn it into something positive.

## Unafraid to ask for help

Pride can be an excellent quality to possess. However, an abundance of pride can lead to stubbornness—which is not conducive to learning. Your protégé should have the ability to determine how much she can do on her own, and when it is time to seek help.

Conversely, you do not want to work with someone who will rely on you completely. There must be a healthy balance of independence and reliance. Awareness of personal limitations is an essential skill for anyone.

This particular quality may be difficult to determine if you haven't had previous contact with a perspective protégé. Part of your "feeling out" may include a short period where you have to evaluate these things.

## Results-driven focus

Both you and your protégé should have clear expectations and results in mind when you enter into a mentoring relationship. Everything you do should work toward a shared goal. Seek out a protégé who has the ability to concentrate and focus. A strong drive is an important quality for success.

Additionally, your protégé should demonstrate willingness to apply what they learn from you to their own career paths. It is useless and frustrating to teach someone who does not intend to use that newfound knowledge. Avoid working with someone who desires only a connection to "important people," and has no real wish to improve or learn.

When observing the prospective protégé, the ability to network is important, but doing it solely to bolster personal position with no relationship building that can improve them personally, or improve the outcomes of your business mission as well as the outcome of the new relations business is bad. A person who does the former is not going to play out well for you, your business, or your business relationships. This kind of protégé will cost you money not make it.

**Willingness to meet regularly**

Be sure the person you choose to work with does not already have an overcrowded schedule. If you cannot meet with your protégé, it is impossible to form a relationship—that goes without saying. Both you and your protégé must be willing to be flexible. This can extend to social life as well: if a candidate insists on putting socialization and entertainment ahead of career in their priorities, you will not be able to gain much ground.

This is a sure sign the prospective charge is not ready for leadership and doesn't understand how to add value to customers, and to your business. They truly don't get the concept that they are responsible for making money, increasing profits, and adding value to your business and your customers.

## Aligning your goals

When it comes to career, you and your protégé should have similar interests and goals. If your primary goal in your career is to effect positive change in your industry, you would not work with someone whose only concern is making money—and if you're in it for the money, you may not enjoy partnering with an altruist.

Of course, this is the extreme ends of both worlds. If you're reading this, you understand business isn't about making money. The money comes from adding real value. So, in all likelihood, your protégé may be at one extreme or the other, and if they can't quickly and easily understand the need for both value to the business, and to the customer, the relationship should move on to someone else.

Before you begin considering candidates, you should be familiar with your personal intentions with regards to becoming a mentor. Answer the following questions truthfully to help yourself determine those qualities you should seek out in a protégé:

- What are your personal reasons for choosing to share your knowledge and experience with a protégé?
- Why did you decide to become a mentor?
- How will becoming a mentor help your career?
- What do you expect your protégé to gain from the relationship?
- What primary benefit do you expect to realize through the relationship?
- Which benefits are secondary?

# Protégé Profits

- Are there any benefits to a protégé that don't matter to you whether you receive them or not?
- How much time do you intend to spend with your protégé?
- Where do you see your protégé after the mentoring process?

Once you have determined your own intentions, you will be in a better position to select a suitable protégé match.

## Background checks—are they really necessary?

You should be familiar with your protégé's background, experiences, and any past instances that may affect your relationship.

In the Navy, I can honestly say I never looked at a person's record before I talked with them and observed them myself. The problem with background records are they can easily mislead you to decisions counter to your personal and business goals.

Third party background checks don't show anything about the real person. They list events. Events that can easily have nothing to do with how your candidate may perform today or the real value they can achieve. These events can also, and frequently are, misstated.

It is in your best interests to treat your search for a protégé as though you are hiring an employee. Request resumes, references, and other pertinent documentation (such as college transcripts for interns) and review the material as part of the process. You should also conduct face-to-face interviews with those candidates who seem a likely fit.

**How to check references**

Personal or professional references should be an important part of your protégé selection process. Since many protégés are entry-level professionals, they may not be able to furnish professional references. However, you can ask for recommendations from college professors, current coworkers, or any other influential people the candidate may have dealt with (such as volunteer program coordinators).

Note: Military people tend to not have a way for you to contact their former commanding officers. It's not a rouse; it is just the nature of the military. People continuously move, and units cease to exist. So instead, use their personnel record. The individual should have a copy of their career evaluations.

When checking references and recommendations, follow the three-step process of **introduction, investigation, and analysis.**

**Introduction**: Identify yourself to the reference (name, position and company) and explain why you're calling. Be sure to stress that the conversation will be confidential. Ask about the reference's relationship with the protégé candidate and try to determine whether the reference is able to give you pertinent information.

**Investigation:** Ask the reference to describe the potential protégé in their own words. You can also ask leading questions: has the candidate demonstrated a willingness to learn? Does he or she seem to desire career advancement? Is he or she easy to get along with? At the end of the conversation, be sure to thank the reference for their time.

**Analysis:** Try to determine how much of the information you obtained from the reference was relevant. It is a good idea to take notes—if not during the conversation, then immediately following. Remain objective, and keep in mind that reference material is someone else's opinion. This should not be the sole factor in your decision-making process. Keep the information you obtained from references so you can compare it with the candidate interview.

### The protégé interview

Face-to-face interviews are an essential step in selecting a protégé. They give you the opportunity to interact with a candidate and allow both of you to test the waters and find out whether you are comfortable with each other. Personal meetings also provide a better sense of style and methodology than you can receive from documents and reference checks.

If you have elected to become a virtual mentor, you should perform a telephone interview. It is difficult to have a true sense of someone's personality strictly through electronic communication; engaging in live conversation will enable you to determine whether you and your protégé will get along well.

Just as in a job interview, you should ask both open and closed questions when talking with a potential protégé. Following are some sample questions you may want to include during the interview*:

# Protégé Profits

Close-ended questions
- How did you hear about this opportunity?
- What are your qualifications?
- What work experience do you have?
- Do you have a college degree?
- What was your major? GPA?
- Have you received any relevant awards or commendations?
- Any hobbies or extracurricular activities that relate to your career?

Open-ended questions
- Why are you seeking a mentor?
- What are your major strengths?
- What do you expect to gain by working with me?
- How do you intend to apply what you learn to your career?
- Name three benefits you would like to receive through this relationship
- Where do you envision your career in five years?
- In what area do you believe you can make the greatest contribution?
- What is your learning style: hands-on? Observatory? A combination?
- What do you believe are the most important qualities you possess?
- What qualities impress you the most in others?
- Name at least one weakness you possess, and tell me how you intend to correct it
- Are you able to accept constructive criticism?
- What are your procedures for handling personal errors?

# Protégé Profits

- How do you work under pressure?
- What would you like to change about this industry?

\* Always avoid asking personal questions, or questions which can only be applied to certain groups of people. For example, do not ask about: marital status, living arrangements, nationality, race, religion, family composition, or social activity. Some of this information may be relevant to discuss with the person you ultimately choose to work with. However, including these questions in an initial interview can make you a potential target for a discriminatory lawsuit. You will need to check your local and national laws to be sure. This varies widely from country to country.

During the interview, pay attention to the way the questions are answered. Does the candidate appear to fumble for responses, or know what to say right away? Are the answers clear and logical? Do they align with your goals? Of course, you should take into account that the interviewee is likely nervous and may stumble at the beginning. However, with a likely match you should have a sense of greater comfort toward the end of the conversation.

Finding the right protégé involves a combination of documentation, reference and interview results, and a certain amount of gut feeling. As with most personal decisions, the process is more art than science. However, establishing a selection procedure allows you to find a common and equitable ground to base your decision on.

## Avoiding lawsuits

Unfortunately, it is easy for well-meaning people to find themselves embroiled in a lawsuit. Most often in mentor-protégé relationships, lawsuits concern slander or libel when one party feels the other is responsible for smearing reputations or creating barriers to success. However, lawsuits can also occur during the selection process if a candidate feels unfairly passed over.

As previously mentioned, your first line of defense against lawsuits is to avoid asking personal questions during the interview process. Other policies, though they are difficult to enforce in a mentor-protégé setting, include invasion of privacy and negligence issues.

Invasion of privacy typically involves the divulgence of confidential information. To avoid invasion of privacy lawsuits, keep in mind that all information exchanged between yourself and a candidate, or yourself and a reference, is not to be shared with others. This includes discussing reference information with a candidate. You should never discuss the details of your interviews with colleagues, reference sources, or other candidates.

Negligence is generally a concern only through an actual hiring process. You should not have to be concerned with negligence when working with a protégé who is already employed by your company, or with an outside entity. However, if you hire a college intern who later damages the company or other employees, you could be held responsible.

# Protégé Profits

Avoiding negligence lawsuits in the case of college interns, you simply need to document your investigation into the candidate's background. You should not hire an intern with references that cannot be checked. Without documentation, you could be at risk for legal recrimination from your company.

**Creating a contract with your protégé**

Once you have selected a protégé, you can avoid misunderstandings—and lawsuits—by creating a contract that defines the expectations, commitment, and objectives on both sides of the relationship. The contract does not need to be an extensive document (in chapter 6, you will learn how to create vision statements that clearly define your working relationship).

The contract simply serves to identify basic rules and allow either party to terminate the relationship in the event things don't work out. Your protégé contract should include:

- Estimated length of time for the mentorship
- Confidentiality disclaimer
- Permissible methods of communication
- Number of hours agreed to devote to the mentorship
- Procedures for requesting additional time
- Necessary steps to dissolve the relationship
- Non-compete agreement, if necessary*

* A non-compete agreement is a clause used to prevent someone, typically an employee, from divulging trade or industry secrets for a certain length of time following

termination of the arrangement. Mentors who intend to share trade secrets or work with a protégé outside their company may wish to include a non-compete agreement to prevent departing protégés from sharing sensitive information with other companies.

Both you and your protégé should possess a hard copy of your contract, signed by both parties and notarized. It is a good idea to have a lawyer peruse your contract to ensure that it is legally binding.

Now I know this ended sounding like a whole lot of scare tactics. Please don't interpret the last part of this chapter this way. Remember, it's important in business for you to protect yourself. There really are people who will do whatever possible to hurt other people when they don't get exactly what they want – whether they earned it or are due it for any legitimate reason or not. I know, as a real business person, you don't let this stop you from adding real value.

# Chapter 5
## Keeping The Communication Lines Open

*"I welcome and seek your ideas, but do not bring me small ideas; bring me big ideas to match our future".*
~Arnold Schwarzenegger~

The method in which you will communicate with each other is an important factor in the mentor-protégé relationship. Your arrangement will vary according to the proximity of your protégé (whether they work for your company, for another company in your area, or are located remotely). It is important to determine not only how you will communicate with your protégé, but also how frequently you will interact.

This chapter will explore the various avenues of communication and assist you in creating a comprehensive information framework that will enhance your mentor-protégé relationship.

### How, Where and When: Communication Basics

### Accessibility

Communication with your protégé can be limited based on several factors, including:

- Job schedule and duties
- Physical location
- External obligations
- Family situation

# Protégé Profits

Flexibility is important here. You and your protégé should discuss each of these areas in order to determine the best ways to accommodate each of your needs.

You've probably come across a few people who have all kinds of rules and limits for you to be able to contact them. There is a place for this. However, to work with a protégé and to be a good mentor, the rules require you have some flexibility, or you will come off as not really caring about your protégé.

## Job schedule and duties

You and your protégé must work around your schedules in order to determine the best times and frequencies for meeting. One of you may work overtime, report to work early, or put in time on weekends on occasion. If you or your protégé work in a career where you are often "on call," such as real estate, medical, or legal, you should establish what constitutes grounds to break off the meeting and how you will reschedule if you lose time.

Remember, if you as a mentor continuously talk about your meeting with your protégé as secondary to any other meetings you have, you can bet your life your charge will think of your mentor-protégé relationship as secondary, or lower.

## Physical location

Depending on the situation, you may or may not be able to physically meet with your protégé. Each scenario provides a separate set of possibilities, and you should determine the rules according to what works for both of you.

# Protégé Profits

In-company mentorships are the simplest in terms of location. You both work at the same company, and you can meet in your office, a conference room, or any accessible area at your place of employment. You can also arrange to meet for lunch if your schedules do not coincide often enough.

External mentorships in which your protégé resides in your area can allow for face-to-face meetings. You may be able to have your protégé come in to your office for meetings, or you can choose a neutral meeting point such as a restaurant, library, or public facility.

Virtual mentorships typically consist of online communication through e-mail and file transfer. You can also set up a private online forum or bulletin board for you and your protégé to exchange ideas through.

Of course, no matter what your physical location, you can always communicate via telephone, fax, and e-mail.

I personally require the charge to have a video camera for video conferencing. There is no reason this is not possible. In fact, most new laptops or desktop computers of any descent quality come with the camera installed. This really helps make your mentorship more personal, and (whether you believe it or not) more profitable.

Why more profitable? Because the more your charge realizes you actually relate with them, the more productive and creative he or she will become.

## External obligations

Business owners and executives often have responsibilities that extend outside of the typical nine-to-five office setting. For example, you may have meetings, seminars, conferences or company events taking place. These external obligations should be considered when scheduling time with your protégé—and your protégé may have other obligations as well.

Your protégé should also be included in these whenever practical. Don't go overboard here, but don't hesitate to use such events as essential development for your charge.

## Regularity

Another important consideration is how often you and your protégé will communicate, and how much time you will spend working together. At the outset of the relationship, you should determine:

- How often you will meet: once or twice per week for a few hours, one or two days a month for extended periods, or any other arrangement that works
- How long the mentorship will last— one or two years is common. But there is fixed amount of time that is the perfect time frame.
- The total amount of interaction time required to meet your goals

You should also figure out ahead of time how you will reschedule in the event of emergencies or disruptions, and whether there are certain blocks of time during the period where either of you will be unavailable for an extended amount of time. It is a good idea to meet as often as possible without placing stress on other areas of your life.

**Primary communication**

It is best if you determine the primary means of communication that will be the least disruptive for both you and your protégé. For example, you may be in a position where you are not able to accept phone calls regularly, in which case e-mail may be your preferred form of communication. Conversely, you may be in a profession which requires you to carry a cell phone to remain in constant contact, and would therefore be able to take phone calls any time.

Be sure to consider the needs of your protégé as well when determining your method of primary communication. The stage they are at now in their career is likely a stage that you have been through yourself, so you will probably understand what works and what does not.

When it comes to virtual mentoring, the primary communication medium should be some kind of personal contact. Email should not be the default.

This doesn't mean you won't use email a lot. Of course you will. However, getting across important instructions, planning out future events, and conveying personal lessons are not done well in emails.

# Protégé Profits

In fact (and you know this is true) because (like me) you have done this: you get an email, it is long, you scan the first sentences or paragraphs and you don't see anything important. So you delete it, or you blow it off.

Days or even weeks later, you find out there was an important task or important details in the last paragraph or sentence, and you never saw it. Am I correct?

Mentors and protégés who work remotely often find creative ways to communicate with one another. The methods include (but are not limited to):

- Forums
- Shared websites or blogs
- E-mail
- Live video conferencing
- Live chat, voice chat, or instant messaging
- Bulletin boards

Remember, virtual mentors should also schedule regular video phone conversations with their protégés in lieu of face-to-face meetings. You should also do a face-to-face if there is any means to make this happen.

**Family situation**

A young bachelor or single female is likely to have more free time than a married person or parent. Single parents in particular will have difficulties in the area of flexibility. Both mentor and protégé should establish meeting times that are convenient to both of them, and do not interrupt or strain other areas of their lives. It is sometimes tricky, but it can be done.

# Protégé Profits

The good news here is that the availability of video conferencing for next to no cost can easily overcome these difficulties. Don't be insensitive to family situations. At the same time, don't let your protégé dictate everything with family situation excuses. You, as the mentor, must establish the acceptable balance, or your charge will soon be in charge.

## Documentation

There are many good reasons to document every aspect of your mentoring program, for both you and your protégé. Conscientious record-keeping is a good practice for any business undertaking. It will help you keep track of your progress, and assist in keeping your program on a focused path.

Documentation is also good for you as a mentor, as you can provide concrete evidence of the work you have done. It is also helpful to be able to review the aspects of your program and identify what worked and what did not—so you can take on a new protégé and improve the process. This is one place where having real, achievable goals pays off for you as the mentor.

The protégé also benefits from documentation. For them, it is also a useful tool for review, as well as a means to provide evidence of having worked with you. They can also track their progress throughout the mentorship and realize how far they have come, and determine whether their original goals are being met.

# Protégé Profits

**Fostering Clear Communication**

Poor communication can lead to misunderstandings, a lack of enjoyment, and failure to transfer knowledge in a meaningful way. This is why communication skills are perhaps the most important step in a successful mentor-protégé relationship.

Following is a guide to clear, concise communication in several forms:

*Conversation skills*
With the increasing reliance on electronic communication, conversation is becoming a lost art form. So don't lose it with your protégé. It can seem difficult to get your point across verbally, and equally hard to understand what someone else is trying to say to you. Relying on electronic, typed media will kill your chance of growing a successful protégé, and realizing the profits you can achieve.

There are several things you can do to improve your verbal communication skills and ensure that you are effectively transferring and receiving information with your protégé:

- Don't be afraid to criticize. Be sure to state what you intend as the end result of your suggestions. Look for common ground to start from, and begin the criticism with a statement like, "I want to help you improve your chances of success in this area/on this project. Let's take a look at what's happened so far." This lets your protégé know that you are offering constructive commentary rather than saying they are inept or worthless.

# Protégé Profits

- Stay positive. If you are communicating criticism or listening to complaints, it is easy for either of you to take things personally. Try to maintain a positive mindset and recognize that when it comes to problems with your mentor- protégé relationship, the disagreement is likely not personal and should be viewed with detachment. Look to the benefit that will

  come from solving the problem, and be sure your protégé understands that you are not attacking him or her. When criticizing, a simple technique that works is to start with something positive, then transition to the criticism, and then conclude with positive actions to be taken. You both will feel good if you practice this as a mentor.
- It is a good idea to rephrase statements you suspect were not meant the way they sounded. For example, if it seems the concern being brought up involves you personally, rather than a business issue, before you become angry or offended try saying, "Did you mean to say XXX?" and reorganize the statement in a less confrontational way. This will diffuse tense emotions on both sides.
- Listening is, by far, the most important aspect of verbal communication. In order to be a good listener, you must remain focused on the conversation. During a face-to-face or telephone meeting with your protégé, be sure to clear your mental plate of other concerns. Trying to think about more than one topic at a time will cloud your focus, and you may miss some of what is being said or take something out of context.

  You are not A.D.D. because you can't focus on multiple

things. No one can do this and remain extremely effective on all things at the same time.

If you're as old as I am while writing this, you know that psychologists and psychiatrists always have a condition or disorder that everyone thinks they have. When I was a kid, it was dyslexia. Then, somewhere around the 1990s, the disorder of the day became A.D.D. Everyone thinks they have it. I'm not saying it can't exist, I'm saying, it has always existed. And if it was as abnormal as you and I are made to believe, then none of us would be able to function.

So the point is, multi-tasking is garbage. Focus on one thing at a time if you want to be effective. Particularly in listening to your protégé. Your charge will know when you aren't listening.

- Don't be afraid to ask questions in order to further understand or clarify the issue; and be ready to admit to not knowing something if you truly don't know. If an issue arises that neither you nor your protégé are familiar with, you can take advantage of the opportunity to learn something new together.

Ask questions simply to show you are listening. If you do this, you will also be surprised at what you discover you did not interpret correctly. Yes, you as the mentor will make mistakes.

# Protégé Profits

There are also certain conversation skills you can develop that will help you to become a better leader. Some approaches are better than others, and when you are attempting to convey knowledge to someone else, there are things you can do to phrase your statements in a way that will leave a lasting impression and not sound harsh or overbearing:

- Avoid using metaphors, stock phrases, or common corporate analogies when explaining concepts or strategies to your protégé. Being a jargon based communicator makes you sound trite, and unattached to the rest of the world.

  Many of today's corporate buzz phrases have become so overused that they are no longer meaningful. Instead, use clear, straightforward language and sincerity when launching into explanations or strategies. Don't use acronyms. They have many different meanings in society, and quickly cause your message to be lost.

- Do not ignore uncertainty, difficulties, or potential failure that may arise in your relationship. Your protégé understands that we are all human, and mistakes happen. It is a mistake to believe that you must present a flawless façade where your protégé is concerned. Allowing your protégé to realize that even you can commit errors will help them persevere through their own mistakes.

  Honestly, if you can't admit error, then you shouldn't be a mentor. There is no such thing as a flawless person. Running your relationship as if there is will only cause loss of respect, and make your protégé feel as if they will never be of any use. In the end, you will lose because the protégé will be less productive, and you already know what that will do to your profits.

- Resist reacting, and respond instead. When your protégé presents you with a question, problem, or challenge, it is tempting to react emotionally. Practice offering a thoughtful response instead. Identify your hot buttons and be ready to diffuse your own emotional reactions when they arise.

  One way to do this is repeating back to your protégé whatever gets you all stirred up. Say something like, "Let me see if I got this right; you think that..." and restate whatever they just said in your own words.

- Avoid making statements or suggestions if you do not intend to follow through. Failure to keep your promises can evoke cynicism and a jaded attitude, which will in turn prove detrimental to the mentor-protégé relationship. Trust will be eroded, and neither of you will benefit from the mentoring process. Your protégé won't feel committed, and guess what will happen to your profits.

When offering constructive criticism, provide specific feedback and examples that illustrate your point. For example, do not just say: "You need to work on your attitude." Rather, cite examples: "If you believe you can't perform well on this project, you won't be able to. It would help if you shift your focus and give it your best shot, instead of complaining that the task is too hard and not trying at all."

- Remember to offer positive feedback as well—but don't get too flowery with your praise. You want to let your protégé know when they're doing a good job, but too much praise can lead to a lack of effort.
- Keep your protégé "in the loop" in regards to developments in the company, your career, and your mentoring process. Offer progress reports periodically to confirm that you are working toward your goals. Lack of communication is just as detrimental as poor communication.

**Personal interface: Your body language**

*"Communication - the human connection - is the key to personal and career success."*
~Paul J. Meyer~

In any communication, the way you present yourself is at least as important, if not more so, than the words you speak. Learning effective body language is an important skill, not only in the mentor-protégé relationship, but for your career in general. Your body language impacts your success because it is totally readable by others.

# Protégé Profits

There are four keys to effective business body language: eye contact, facial expression, handshake technique and posture. Each of these keys possesses a set of rules that will help you make the best impression on your protégé as well as your colleagues, industry personnel, and supervisors.

### *Eye contact*
Maintaining eye contact during a conversation is critical for two reasons. It lets the other person know you're paying attention, and it allows you to read what they are saying, even if their meaning is different from the words they speak.

You should make eye contact as soon as you begin a conversation. Of course, if you are attempting to engage someone, eye contact can attract attention before a conversation begins. Continue throughout the exchange, even when you are saying goodbye.

One thing to note is that prolonged direct eye contact can be disconcerting. Instead of staring straight at the other person's eyes, try to concentrate on the point between the nose and lips. Remain focused but not necessarily sharpened, and do not let your gaze drift downward. Proper eye contact can seem something of an art form, but keep practicing!

It is o.k. to look away, and break what seems like a stare. Maintaining eye contact does not mean staring down your protégé. However, never looking at your charge shows a distinct lack of interest.

# Protégé Profits

It is a good idea to maintain eye contact for 70 to 80 percent of the conversation. This avoids appearing disinterested or, conversely, overbearing. Glancing away occasionally is acceptable, but do not look over the other person's shoulder—this can indicate that you're looking for someone more interesting to talk to.

Of course, these numbers are really just for those of you that have to have numbers. You can feel if it's comfortable or not, so don't get focused on the numbers.

*Facial expression*
A smile is a powerful expression. Smiles can create a positive and upbeat environment; convey interest and excitement, or show empathy and concern. Your smile can enhance your image and help you appear interesting and engaging; a person worthwhile to converse with.

However, smiles can be overused or appear phony. It is a good idea to reserve smiling for conversation, rather than enter a room with a smile already plastered on. Using smiles sincerely and genuinely will bolster a professional image.

Everyone knows when you are just painting on a smile, whether you think so or not. If you are a habitual "fake" smiler, everyone knows it except you.

*Handshake technique*

The business handshake is a widely accepted form of nonverbal communication. Many people will either consciously or unconsciously judge you by the way you perform this social ritual. It is generalized that men have stronger, firmer handshakes than women, but this is not always the case. Women can also develop firm handshakes that convey authority and confidence.

Familiarizing yourself with common types of handshakes will help you improve your nonverbal communication and become better at interpreting others:

The **sandwich or politician's handshake** is fairly self-explanatory. This involves engulfing the other person's hand in both of yours. To most people it is uncomfortable to have to receive this type of handshake; it is an invasion of private space, and should be used only with people you know well on a personal level.

The **dead fish handshake** happens when the hands are wet, usually for one of two reason: nervous sweat, or the transfer of a cold beverage from the dominant hand in order to shake. In either case, gripping a dead fish is an unpleasant experience and will not convey a good impression. If your hands sweat, be sure to rub your palm lightly on a napkin, tablecloth, or even your pants before accepting a handshake. Also, if you are in a situation where handshakes are expected, remember to hold drinks with your non-dominant hand.

The **controlling handshake** occurs when the hands meet and one person purposefully maneuvers to the top. This indicates the controller wants to be in charge of the conversation.

# Protégé Profits

The **limp-fingered handshake** most often occurs with women, who tend to extend only their fingers rather than the entire hand. This not only appears weak, it can also be painful when the fingers are gripped in a forceful handshake. It is important to extend your full hand horizontally and flat, without cupping it.

There is also what I call the **"dead man's" handshake**. I remember well when I first met one of my peers in the Navy. He was a big guy. You expected when he shook your hand that it would be very firm, and maybe even hurt.

Instead, he holds his hand out. You clasp each other. Only he never really clasps you. He takes no grip at all. This kind of handshake is very unnerving. Don't do it. You will actually make your encounter think there is something wrong with you.

What constitutes a good handshake? You should hold the other person's hand firmly and shake (not pump) no more than three times. Maintain constant eye contact, and keep a positive outlook. Always act as though, no – always be genuinely pleased to meet the person.

### *Posture*
First impressions are still important, and your posture says a lot about you before you get the chance to speak. The way you carry yourself has a significant impact on the way others perceive you. If you slouch, droop your shoulders, or sag in place, it can project the idea that you're not sure of yourself.

Proper business posture includes:

- Stomach in
- Chest out
- Head up
- Shoulders back

The way you stand can turn people away, or command respect. It also affects your confidence level. You can feel grounded and balanced if you stand with your feet planted firmly, six to eight inches apart, with one slightly in front of the other.

Additionally, you can reveal through your posture whether or not you want others to approach you. Two people engaged in a conversation who are forming a rectangle (squarely facing each other with neither turned to one side) have effectively closed off their space and don't want to be interrupted.

If one or both members of the conversation are angled away with feet pointing outward, like two sides of a triangle, at least one of them is open to others joining them. People unconsciously recognize this, so your positioning is key as to whether others join in with you or not.

**Better written communication**

Much of your communication with your protégé will be written, particularly if you use e-mail frequently or are acting as a virtual mentor. When crafting written correspondence such as letters, reports, and progress records, there are rules you can apply to ensure effective communication. E-mail writing involves some of the same principles, but there are many differences in method and execution.

# Protégé Profits

**Written correspondence**

Effective written communication is a difficult task for many, particularly when writing is not part of their regular job responsibilities. Clear business writing is an important skill to master. During the course of the mentor-protégé relationship, you will likely write reports, documentation for your protégé to study, and letters of recommendation. Each of these documents should be formulated with clarity in mind.

Strive to keep your written business communication free of clutter and extraneous ideas. Wordy writing tends to distract rather than impress and can easily muddle your point. It is acceptable to use a professional level of language, but try to steer clear of using buzzwords, clouded metaphors, and "hype" in your business communication. Get to the point as soon as possible.

The tone of your written communication should be professional but courteous. Engaging business writing addresses a single reader. Do not be afraid to use the pronoun "you" in your writing; this brings a sense of immediacy and connection, and allows the reader to identify with your message. When you use words like "one" or "those" instead of "you" people instantly interpret it to mean "you."
If one doesn't believe me, then what did one think when reading this sentence? You should be convincing and complete when conveying written ideas, and not be deceptive, intentionally or not.

## Electronic etiquette

Effective e-mail communication was practically a lost art at its inception. E-mail equates with speed, and a majority of e-mails reflect that with poor spelling and grammar, incomplete thoughts, and unclear messages.

One of the often unrealized advantages of improving your e-mail communication is that it encourages others to do the same when replying to you. If you send sloppy e-mails, do not answer promptly, or come across as vague or harsh, you can expect to receive the same communication from others.

Here are some pointers that will help you sharpen your e-mail etiquette:
- Remember that e-mail is by no means confidential. Refrain from including personal or sensitive information in electronic communication.
- Think before you send. E-mail is a fast form of communication, but you still do not have to dash off a quick reply and forget about it. Reread what you've written before you send the message: is your intention clear? Will the recipient understand what you're saying, or can your message be misinterpreted?
- Use proper grammar and spelling. It may be easier and faster not to bother with trifles like punctuation and capitalization, but your message will be difficult to read and may cause the recipient to not bother trying to figure out what you meant to say. Again the recipient will think you don't know anything about writing, and the response will reflect it.

# Protégé Profits

- Make your subject line active rather than passive. Instead of sending an e-mail with the subject "Project update" or "Status report", state what is included and what action you wish the recipient to take. For example: "Information on the Smith project you wanted" or "Need your input on the status of this account." This will encourage the recipient to read and respond to your message.
- Messages in the body of an e-mail should be short and concise. Because of the way most e-mail programs appear on a screen, it is difficult to read long or complicated data, such as reports, in a reduced area. Longer electronic messages should be sent as attachments.
- Never type in ALL CAPS. It looks like you're SHOUTING AT THE READER. If you want to emphasize a point, do so through your use of language, or with bold or italicized typeface. However, be aware that some formatting does not transfer properly between e-mail programs—another good reason to ensure your message is clear and concise. This does not mean to use all lower case. This looks "stupid." I'm guessing you don't want to look stupid!
- Once again: always double-check your message before you click on Send. Check for spelling and grammar, a compelling subject line, and clear expression of the information you're sending. Virtually every email program of any minor quality has a spell checker. Use it, or pay the price

- Finally, if you want to get the action you desire from the email, only put one action in it. Reflect on this; have you ever sent an email to a technical support place with 3 or 4 problems in the email? How many got fixed or were addressed in the response? Don't lie to yourself here. You know you frequently get only the first one, maybe two addressed. The others are never even seen by the recipient, and thus aren't addressed in the response.

Are you getting the picture here? If you want consistent, complete responses to your emails, then only put one main action in the email. If you are going to do more, you must make it clear in the first sentence that the email contains a certain number of tasks.

## Creating a schedule

Sit down with your protégé and compare schedules to determine the best times for meeting and working together. You may want to prepare spreadsheets which you can overlap to find when you both have free time. For more challenging schedules, alternative times to consider arranging meetings might be:

- Early mornings
- Lunch breaks
- Evenings
- Weekends
- Minor national holidays

## Protégé Profits

Another good strategy in regards to scheduling is to determine goal markers that should be met after certain periods of time, and then scheduling enough time to meet those goals. I'll even go so far to say that this is required. Without clear goals, measuring progress will be next to impossible. There is no point to your relationship, if you can't measure progress.

Be sure to note the communication rules you and your protégé have set forth on the schedule. For example, if your protégé has questions between meetings, indicate whether they should give you a call, or simply send an e-mail which you can answer when you have time.

Remember; don't make your protégé feel totally secondary in everything. If you do, the productivity you get in return will be reflected clearly; most likely in your profits from your protégé.

Both of you should have a copy of your schedule, and know how much notice you should attempt to give if you must cancel or reschedule a meeting. With the exception of true emergencies, last-minute cancellations are disrespectful when enacted from either party. You should extend the same respect in regards to your protégé's time as you expect to receive.

# Protégé Profits

# Chapter 6
## Working Side By Side

It will be beneficial to do some planning before you begin your relationship with a protégé so that both sides are clear on what is expected of them, and what you and your charge should expect to gain during the process.

This chapter will walk you through the process of establishing the relationship and working with your protégé toward a mutual, beneficial goal.

**Stages of a mentorship**

Typically, the mentor-protégé relationship has four separate and distinct stages:

- Orientation: During the first three to six months, depending on the frequency of interaction, you and your protégé are getting to know each other. This period lays the foundation for the relationship. You will be developing expectations, building trust, and preparing to learn from each other. You will be feeling each other out.
- Education: The middle stage of a mentorship is generally the most rewarding for both you and your protégé. At this stage, solid trust has developed, bringing a greater sense of confidence. Both you and your protégé will feel comfortable challenging one another and offering ideas freely. This is when the creativity flows, and the advantages to your business, and to your protégé flourish.
- Dissolution: Mentoring relationships can last one to

- two years, or until your protégé feels ready to move.
- Dissolution: Mentoring relationships can last one to two years, or until your protégé feels ready to move on without you. When you reach dissolution, it is important to step back and discuss with your protégé how the relationship should continue.
- Redefinition: When the mentoring process ends, you and your protégé can interact as equals on a more casual basis. You will have established a foundation that will allow for a long and continually prosperous business relationship. If you have done your part well, this will mean even more business for you in the future.

You can expect to put forth the most effort during the orientation and education stages of the mentorship. I think this may seem obvious, but just like in mentoring, don't assume anything is known if it's never been said between you. If the process is successful, dissolution and redefinition of the relationship become natural steps for the conclusion.

**Pitfalls of mentoring**

As with any relationship, mentor-protégé partnerships do not always succeed. It can be frustrating to enter a relationship, only to discover that you are not as compatible as you thought or that, for whatever reason, things just aren't going to work out. However, there are things you can to do give your mentor relationship the best chances for success.

The following presents the most common problems of mentorships and the best possible solutions for avoiding those problems.

**Problem: You or your protégé possess unrealistic expectations.**

*Solution:* Make sure you are clear about what your protégé should expect to receive during the mentoring process. If it appears that more will be expected, do not agree to the relationship. You should not be expected to give more than you are prepared to offer. This also applies to your expectations of your protégé's performance. Be prepared to discover what the protégé can offer you, and do not expect more than what is agreed upon.

Establishing realistic expectations and understandings up front will get you the right person, and also have a high probability of creating a protégé who out performs your desires.

**Problem: Confidentiality is breached on either side of the relationship.**

*Solution:* Work to develop trust between yourself and your protégé. Be sure that your protégé understands what happens between you should be treated as confidential, and be prepared to extend that courtesy in return. Creating a contract with a non-compete clause, as discussed in a previous chapter, is a good way to avoid breaches of confidentiality and to ensure that recourse is in place should a breach occur.

Simply being clear and doing what you say generally brings out a similar performance from your protégé. In business relationships, the juniors work hard to mimic their seniors in every way you can imagine – quite literally!

# Protégé Profits

**Problem: The mentor and protégé match is not good.**
*Solution:* Don't rush through the selection process. Take your time in evaluating potential protégés to ensure the best chance of choosing one you can work with successfully. You should never leap at the opportunity to mentor someone on the basis of a recommendation or request. Always investigate before agreeing to take on a protégé.

You can even invite your potential charge to join you for a few days as part of a weeding out process. It's amazing what a few short hours will reveal.

## Defining goals

During the orientation stage, you and your protégé should each have clear goals in mind. These goals will likely shift in scope and direction as you move through the process, but it is helpful to create a roadmap from which to start.

The goals you set should be incrementally achievable by both you and your protégé. They should be a series of small steps, leading to a bigger, broader goal. Using small steps makes the whole process measurable, and creates multiple points of success during the relationship. It also helps you map out where the protégé can add the most to your business and success.

## Your goals

Knowing what you expect to contribute and take away from the relationship can assist you in formulating a successful mentoring strategy. In the initial stage, you should determine the following:

# Protégé Profits

- What experiences have you had that will allow you to impart the necessary knowledge?
- What aspects of your industry should your protégé learn more about in order to become successful?
- How far do you anticipate taking your protégé? Will you attempt to assist him in reaching your level? Do you want to help her surpass you?
- To what extent do you expect your protégé to participate in your work? What clearances or permissions does he require for a meaningful experience?
- What do you expect to learn from your protégé? Are there any new developments in your industry in which she may be knowledgeable?
- Will your protégé react better to a nurturing approach or a "tough love" method? Which attitude is generally more prevalent in your industry?
- What was the most beneficial advice you received during your career, and how will you communicate this to your protégé?
- What contacts should you introduce your protégé to? Which events should she attend? Where can he find further career assistance?
- What can you realistically expect your protégé to accomplish during the mentor relationship?
- What form should information take: written notes, hands-on practice, actual involvement and participation, or a combination of these?

Remember, each of these items can have multiple goals to achieve in incremental steps. So spend some time thinking about this. You and your business will reap the rewards, along with your protégé.

# Protégé Profits

**Your protégé's goals**

Encourage your protégé to determine his or her own set of goals for the relationship. This will allow for greater participation and a higher degree of interaction, as well as smoother exchanges of ideas.

**Questions your protégé should answer include:**

- To what extent do you expect to be involved in your mentor's career responsibilities?
- What would you most like to learn from your mentor?
- Which contacts and industry events are you most interested in becoming involved with?
- What is your ultimate career goal: to reach the level of your mentor, or to surpass it?
- What experiences have you had that will benefit the relationship?
- What is your strongest learning style: written communication, vocal instruction, hands-on learning, or a combination of these?
- Do you react better to a nurturing approach or a "tough love" mentality? What drives you to excel?
- What knowledge and information can you offer your mentor?
- Which areas of your industry are you most interested in learning more about?
- How much time and effort are you willing to invest in the relationship?

When you have both completed your goals, share them with each other so you can establish common ground and decide which areas are of primary importance. You can utilize your goals to help you plan your mentoring path and arrive at your intended destination.

## Creating a personal vision statement

> *"Leadership is the capacity to translate vision into reality".*
> ~Warren G. Bennis~

Creating a personal vision statement can help you remain focused on your objectives and tailor your mentoring relationship to suit your vision. What is a personal vision statement? A personal vision statement is a refined, concise statement of your goals.

Both you and your protégé should develop personal vision statements to guide you through the relationship and toward your ultimate career objectives.

## Defining your vision

Your personal vision statement should cover not only what you hope to achieve from your career, but from life in general. A personal vision statement can be a powerful tool for goal definition and focus.

Why is it important to define your vision? One reason is that without it, others can manipulate your vision and lead you to believe you desire whatever it is they desire for you. It is better to be directed by your own goals, rather than the expectations of others.

I lacked a personal vision statement in my Navy career. My goals were all professional, so I couldn't really exist in a fulfilled way outside of the work space. Your personal vision statement makes it possible to make it all fit together for both you and your protégé.

Your vision should include what you would like to see from yourself, as well as from the world around you. Whether your ultimate goal is as simple as adopting a healthier attitude and perspective, or as lofty as changing the world, your vision allows you to hone your efforts toward a single purpose. This definition can help you and your protégé determine where your efforts are best spent during the mentoring process.

Defining your vision requires concentration. You should give serious thought to your goals and your wishes. Choose a quiet, uninterrupted place and time to outline your answers to the following questions:

- What values are most important to you? Family, faith, success, recognition, honesty, money?
- List the issues you care deeply about. If you had the time and the means, what would you do in regards to these issues?
- What three things would you do if you had unlimited financial resources?
- What are your strengths—in what areas do you excel?
- What brings you the most happiness? Include emotions and external events here.
- What are the things you truly enjoy doing? This can apply to both your career and your personal life.
- Recall the three best moments of your life. What was it about them that brought you joy? Who was involved in these moments? Were any of them solo efforts?
- What are you doing now that you would like to stop doing, or do less?

## Writing the vision statement

Once you have brainstormed to define your vision, it is then time to pull that information together and create a concise statement that reflects your ultimate goal.

You should include several areas of your life in your personal vision statement. The statement should be written in present tense, and reflect the way you visualize yourself as if you already have achieved these things.

Do not limit yourself to the mundane or apparently unachievable. With your personal vision statement, you should feel free to reach for the stars and believe that nothing is impossible. If you cannot visualize yourself actually doing or living your vision, then your chances of ever living that vision pretty much stink right from the start.

One way to create a personal vision statement is to distill the information you generated in the previous exercise into several short statements, including:

- The main things that motivate you and bring you personal satisfaction
- Your greatest strengths, abilities, and personality traits
- At least two things you can start doing now that will bring you heightened satisfaction in your life

Try to write your personal vision statement in fifty words or less. This brevity allows you to focus on what matters most to you and align your actions with your goals. Here is a sample personal vision statement:

"I am working in a career I love and earning a sufficient salary to live comfortably. I have a positive outlook and I can laugh at myself. I have plenty of time to spend with my family. I am helping others advance their careers, and taking art classes".

This is an example of a mundane personal vision statement. So please don't copy it. I'm simply showing you how to use the present tense.

Here's another:

"I am making a radical difference in the lives of many people through the products I create and the training I provide. I am creating endless wealth and prosperity for myself, my family and all of my business clients. I have a totally positive and clear view of life, enjoying vacations when and where I want them, and bringing joy and health to my family".

Remember, it doesn't matter if you actually have achieved this yet. You only need to possess the ability to visualize yourself in this way. If you live the vision, the vision will become real for both you and your protégé.

## Effective meetings

Your primary interaction with your protégé will be through some type of meeting – face-to-face or virtual. Holding effective meetings is an important step in the mentoring process, and a key to ensuring the overall success of the mentor-protégé relationship.

What are the elements of an effective meeting? It is likely that you have participated in, or even led meetings during the course of your employment, or the running of your business. One way to ensure smooth mentor-protégé meetings is to analyze meetings you have attended in the past and determine what has worked and what could have been improved. You can then apply these findings to your own meetings.

If the meetings you ran or attended were boring, then don't copy them. Figure out what makes them boring, and do something to make your future meetings better.

Here are more tips to holding effective meetings with your protégé:

**Plan ahead of time**

You and your protégé will likely have time constraints when it comes to personal meetings. It is a good idea to ensure that the time you do have is used as effectively as possible. Before each meeting, take the time to determine what will be covered during your time. Plan a tentative schedule that outlines each topic and the approximate length of time you expect to spend on each one. Be sure to leave a bit of a buffer to handle unexpected issues or delays. Don't be robotic about your agenda.

**Establish communication protocol**

Though it is not necessary to require your protégé to raise his hand when asking a question, you should establish some ground rules for discussion. For example, you can agree not to interrupt each other when one of you is speaking; or hold questions until the conclusion of a particularly involved presentation. Another good protocol is in regards to criticism. Make it a point, for both you and your protégé, to always state the positive before the negative. Express what you like about an idea or action before you criticize what does not work. This will avoid potentially wasteful disagreements.

Remember the difference between criticism and complaining. Criticism offers solutions. Complaining does not. It's very clear when someone is just complaining.

### Encourage prepared and spontaneous questions

Let your protégé know what you intend to discuss at each meeting ahead of time, and encourage them to prepare a list of questions on the topics. Any questions that are not answered during the course of the discussion can then be addressed easily. You should also prepare questions you would like to ask your protégé regarding progress or ideas. However, do not limit the questioning to prepared lists.

Encourage your protégé to ask any questions generated by the presented information, and be prepared to give thoughtful, reflective answers. Spontaneous questions can often open the floor for new ideas that will benefit you both.

### Record the proceedings

It is important to remember what you discuss with your protégé at each meeting. Taking notes is a good idea; however, it is often difficult to do so in a one-on-one situation. A better idea may be to have a small digital recorder to record everything. Encourage your protégé to bring one as well, or allow him to borrow your recording and take notes or make a copy. If you were smart, and used a digital recorder, then email it, or create a private podcast blog to share your recording.

**Encourage time for reflection**

After each meeting, both you and your protégé should take some time to consider what you have learned and digest the new information. You should enter this period of reflection as soon as possible following the meeting, while it is still fresh in your mind. Make note of your reflections and outline possibilities for new discussions, new questions, and things which can be improved for your next meeting. You may wish to involve your protégé in the planning process for your meetings as well.

**Making time for mentoring: the balancing act**

I know that you are aware of the fact that it is important to balance your work life and your personal life in order to avoid stress. Adding the responsibility of a mentor relationship can cause strain if you are not prepared to integrate the additional time with your current lifestyle.

There are many ways to find time for mentoring, and many reasons to make the effort. Mentoring is a rewarding and profitable experience; it is to your benefit to juggle your schedule and make the time to nurture a protégé.

Having someone to "fill your shoes" will make your life amazingly more abundant in more ways than just financially. Here are some time management tips for the mentoring process:

- Do not commit to more time than you can realistically handle.
- Consider combining your career responsibilities with your mentoring process. If you are attending an industry event or company meeting that would benefit your protégé, find out whether you can bring them along.
- It is easy for you or your protégé to become frustrated with a lack of quality time. Try to remain as flexible as possible and learn to take advantage of the time you do have. Make it a rule to reserve personal conversation for e-mail or other casual communications, and only discuss business during face-to-face meetings.
- If you have personal activities that take up time, consider cutting back on them for the duration of the formal mentoring process—make a few less trips to the gym, or downplay your commitments to outside groups or organizations.
- Boundaries are important and should be observed on both sides. Be sure to make it clear to your protégé when you are and are not available, and expect to do the same for them.

If you truly desire to make a difference in another person's life through mentoring, you will find the time to take on this enriching challenge.

**Drawing the line**

In a mentor-protégé relationship, it is easy to do too much for your protégé. Keep in mind that you are enabling your protégé to succeed on their own merits. Doing too much for them can allow them to rely on your support instead of turning to themselves and striving to perform better.

Though you should certainly attempt to give your protégé every advantage, there are areas in which you can take things too far. Here are some common mistakes mentors make in extending their services:

**Becoming a personal counselor**
Mentors and protégés work closely together toward a common goal. Therefore, it is only natural that some personal exchanges will occur. You will likely get to know about each others' families, hobbies, and personal interests outside of your careers. It is certainly important to be involved to some extent, as part of your task as a mentor is to assist your protégé in balancing work and personal affairs.

However, there are certain personal issues in which you should not become involved. If your protégé is experiencing marital difficulties, mental health problems, substance abuse struggles, or other potentially damaging hardships, you should not offer to coach or advice regarding them.

One step in avoiding too much personal involvement is to set clear boundaries at the outset of the mentor-protégé relationship. Discuss the fact that there are certain issues which should not be brought into the workplace. Let your protégé know that you do care, but you cannot offer extensive personal guidance.

If your protégé brings a massive personal struggle to your attention, you should suggest other avenues for resolution, such as a company counselor or psychiatrist, mental help hotline, or community intervention program. For serious issues in which your protégé demonstrates the potential to harm himself or someone else, you should not hesitate to report the issue to authorities.

In my long life of training and mentoring, my single biggest weakness was not saying "no" often enough, or even at all. Here's what happens when you become too easily dependable for anything and everything: people start believing they can and should ask you for everything or anything they feel like. What's worse, you lose the ability to create an atmosphere of reciprocity. You absolutely must say no, particularly in the areas discussed in this chapter for setting boundaries.

You cannot have your mentor thinking he or she can get anything they want from you. If they do, you will no longer be the mentor. You will simply be a pawn.

Does this sound harsh? Too bad, it's real, and this is about reality. You must say no, and be firm about it. On rare occasions, you may break the "no," but it must be very rare indeed.

**Offering financial support**
Some protégés may ask their mentors to buy a product, invest capital in a business enterprise, or even help pay personal bills. Though your protégé may actually be in dire financial straits, or the venture proposed may seem worthwhile, providing financial support is not a good idea.

# Protégé Profits

Financial investments change the dynamics of the mentor-protégé relationship. If you have a monetary stake in an enterprise run by your protégé, you are no longer a mentor; you are a partner. Also, when it comes to personal bills, if you agree to help out, your protégé will very likely become dependent on you. This is exactly what you don't want.

If you are asked to invest in a project or otherwise offer financial assistance during the course of a mentoring relationship, it is a good idea to refuse gently, explain why you must refuse, and offer to discuss the possibility at the conclusion of the relationship (if the venture is something you believe will succeed).

**"Working" for your protégé**
Your protégé may ask you to perform tasks for them that would be better suited accomplishing themselves. Examples of these include writing a resume, question fellow employees about the protégé's job performance, or complete applications for scholarships or grants. These are skills your protégé should be developing for themselves.

If your protégé approaches you with such a request, you can bow out gracefully. State that you are glad she has faith in your abilities, but explain that it would be to her advantage to take on the task herself. You can offer assistance and guidance, but do not complete the task in your protégé's stead.

# Protégé Profits

# Chapter 7
## Time To Call It A Night

*"Nobody talks of entrepreneurship as survival, but that's exactly what it is and what nurtures creative thinking".*
~Anita Roddick~

The conclusion of the mentor-protégé relationship should be a shared realization of projected goals, marked by the successful completion of one phase in a long-term relationship. In fact, it should be a celebration!

Of course, the dynamics of the relationship will change upon dissolution of the mentor-protégé roles. Your protégé is embarking on a journey toward a successful career. As a mentor, you can take pride in witnessing your protégé spread their wings and soar on their own.

A successful exit strategy can be compared to the graduation. It's a big event well worth celebrating. You and your protégé should engage in a review of the mentoring process, wrap up any unfinished business, and create plans for the future of the changed relationship, and of course, don't forget the party(!)

**Meeting goals**
At this stage, it is a good idea to return to the original goals you and your protégé established at the outset of the relationship. Have your goals been met? Is your protégé in a position to grow without your direct guidance? Goals may be met directly or indirectly through the mentoring process. An extensive comparison of before-and-after situations can show you whether the mentorship has been successful.

# Protégé Profits

Answer the following questions in regards to your goals for both you and your protégé:

- Has your protégé made any noticeable advancements in his career? If so, what were they?
- In which specific skill areas has your protégé progressed the most? The least? What should he concentrate on at this point?
- Is it easy to envision your protégé advancing in his career and becoming a success at this point?
- Has the relationship progressed on a generally upward slope?
- Have you taught your protégé everything you can about your industry?
- Did your goals change over the course of the mentorship? If so, were the new goals met sufficiently?
- Do you have a greater sense of confidence in both your abilities and the abilities of your protégé as compared to the outset of the relationship?
- What were the greatest challenges your protégé encountered and how did she meet them?
- Do you feel you are in a better position, either personally or professionally, as a result of the mentorship?
- What were the greatest challenges you encountered during the mentoring process, and how did you meet them?
- Does your protégé have access to higher levels of influence in your industry? What are the specific connections you have helped her make?

## Protégé Profits

- What were the most important things you learned during the mentoring process?

Feedback is also an important part of the exit strategy. At this stage, it is important to continue clear communication. Let your protégé know not only how successful the relationship has been, but why it has been successful. Your feedback will mean a lot to your protégé, and will help him or her continue to strive for improvement and excellence. Your feedback should be a review of the personal vision statement, looking to see where you and your mentor actually are with respect to the vision.

Here are some pointers on giving constructive feedback:

- Ask questions, and listen carefully to the answers. Some of your conceptions regarding the process may be a result of miscommunication, and a simple question can often clear up misgivings.
- Always start and end with the positive. Opening your feedback with negative commentary will sting, even if you end on a positive note. If there are problems you would like to address, be sure you cushion the potential blow with positive feedback.
- Communicate your intentions in pointing out problems or errors. Let your protégé know why you believe the problem occurs, and what you think should be done to correct it.
- Make your tone respectful and genuinely interested. You are not ending the relationship; you are merely shifting gears. You and your protégé can continue to benefit from one another's input and support.

- Keep it clear and concise. Back up your comments with actual examples from your notes, reports, or recollections gathered during the course of the mentoring relationship.

You should also ask for feedback from your protégé on the mentoring process. Ask your protégé which aspects of the process worked and which did not, and solicit suggestions on what could be done to improve the process. This will help you in the future, and enable you to take on another protégé, if you desire.

**Keeping in touch**

The best mentor-protégé relationships extend long beyond the actual mentoring process. Your protégé may continue to work at your company; in which case you will likely become colleagues or partners and continue to work together. If your protégé does not work for your company, you may decide to assist them with career placement. Or, you may simply agree to keep in touch and fill each other in on the details of your careers.

Your protégé could easily end up in a position to bring you more business, and help you grow your business from the outside. So don't lose the relationship. Let it grow.

You and your protégé should discuss the framework for future communications. Since the relationship has changed, you will not need formal documentation or a contract, so this arrangement should be casual and agreeable to both of you.

# Protégé Profits

**Moving on**

Once you have reviewed the process, it is time to wrap up any loose ends and finalize things. Congratulations are in order for both yourself and your protégé: you have successfully completed an important and rewarding experience, and gained new life skills that will help you succeed.

It is a good idea to celebrate and commemorate the occasion of your "graduation." You and your protégé might consider having dinner together, or taking the time to have a relaxed and meaningful conversation reflecting on the progress you have made. In any event, it is a time for celebration on a job well done.

Even better, invite him and his family to join you to celebrate. Make this special. Ensure your mentor knows they really have accomplished something in life.

**Key points to consider:**
- *Method of communication*: If you kept in touch via telephone during the mentoring process, you and your protégé may agree to communicate primarily via e-mail in order to be able to respond at your convenience. Establish casual rules governing phone calls and personal visits to be sure neither of you interrupts the other, and keep the relationship comfortable.
- *Physical location:* If you and your protégé are near each other now, will that situation change? Does your protégé intend to relocate?
- *Level of activity*: Both you and your protégé may experience increases in your respective workloads

following the dissolution of the mentorship. This will limit the frequency of your exchanges, but you should still endeavor to keep in touch.
- *The new purpose:* What will you now expect to derive from the relationship? You and your protégé may simply be interested in remaining friends; or you may be able to continue assisting each other. Determine what goals, if any, you would like to achieve from this point on and how you will go about reaching them.

Working with a protégé is an exciting experience that can build lasting relationships and allow you to touch another person's life. Many great friendships have been formed during mentor-protégé relationships, and many of the most successful business leaders credit their mentors with their achievements. Why not add your name to the list of exalted mentors?

I know my career in the Navy teaching, mentoring, and leading had one big disappointment. The people you mentored constantly got reassigned to new duty stations. It was nearly impossible to keep up with them.

This was a great personal loss. The names ring loud and clear in my head. To this day, I wonder where they have gone, and what they have achieved.

Don't lose contact! It's very important to you and your protégé whether either of you is willing to admit it or not. Be real, and stay in contact. It will be rewarding and profitable for both of you.

# Chapter 8
## A Squadron of Protégés

The enthusiastic mentor can take on more than one protégé at a time because mentoring is such a flexible and customizable experience. It is quite possible to have multiple protégés without diluting the quality of the mentoring process, and without making yourself crazy keeping up with them.

In fact, as a squadron commanding officer, this was definitely the case. As a leader, it was my job to ensure I molded the right people to replace me in the future. In a two year stint as a commanding officer, I was responsible for "creating" (for lack of a better word) four future commanding officers. The more senior you are in your organization, the more you are responsible for creating futures.

Good qualities to possess if you plan to have more than one protégé are:

- Experience in a variety of areas
- Well-developed social skills
- A strong desire to make a radical difference in your life, and the lives of others.
- An established set of core materials and knowledge bases
- Excellent organizational skills
- A flexible work and personal schedule
- Conviction and commitment to the mentoring mindset
- The ability to multitask and meet deadlines.

(Remember, multi-tasking constantly is not desirable. It's the ability to use multi-tasking effectively when it's appropriate.)

# Protégé Profits

If these qualities describe you, then you may want to consider multiple mentorships. There are several different strategies you can employ in working with more than one protégé.

## Diversifying: Different protégés for different purposes

Many business professionals and business owners have experience in more than one area. You may have held several positions within your company, or worked with a variety of companies in different capacities. If this is the case, you can select multiple protégés with interests that match your diverse experience.

To begin this process, familiarize yourself with those areas in which you have experience, and identify those beginners who would be most interested in learning from you. In the business world, there are many paths and branches to choose from at the start of a career, and each path leads to a new destination with more choices.

As an experienced professional, you can help protégés determine their own path and get them on their way. When you are running multiple protégés in different areas, be sure that you are consistently clear in your communication. Devise a method of distinguishing skills and knowledge that should be passed on in each individual case.

It is helpful to be aware of all the possible paths to success within your industry, even those you have not chosen to take. In this way, you can help someone whose goals may differ from yours, without seeming presumptuous.

# Protégé Profits

## Part time mentoring

Most mentoring, as a rule, is part time. Particularly for those whose companies do not offer a formal, structured mentoring program, mentors often work on a volunteer basis and must find time outside of their regular job duties to develop a protégé. The good news is that more organizations are realizing the benefits of offering a mentor program, and are taking steps to initiate them within the company.

The best part time mentoring programs are structured with the needs of both the mentor and the protégé in mind. Mandatory part time mentoring when no consideration is given to the workload of the mentor causes undue stress, and can result in a minimally effective mentor relationship that often causes more harm than good. Some companies offer partial work release for those who agree to become mentors. This allows the mentor to concentrate fully on the protégé, and keeps him from having to take necessary time away from other activities.

If your company offers a part-time mentoring program that includes work release qualifications, you can take on multiple protégés by donating some of your off-work time. This option is best for those who do not have a crowded social calendar, but it can be done in nearly any circumstance. You may simply choose to offer an hour or two of your time twice a month to a protégé who has the basic components for success in place, and only requires a bit of your influence and knowledge to soar.

College interns are another viable option for part-time mentoring. Because interns are expected to share in the mentor's workload, the relationship does not detract from the mentor's responsibilities. If your budget allows for hiring multiple college interns—or if you can solicit them for free—you might consider taking advantage of the extra help while simultaneously offering young people a better chance at success.

**Group mentoring**

This option is becoming more popular as the resource of available time dwindles for most busy professionals. Group mentoring, as the name suggests, involves instructing several protégés simultaneously who possess similar goals and objectives. There have been arguments for and against group mentoring: those in favor of the process state the ability to extend the benefits of mentoring to a greater number of young people, while those opposed cite deterioration of quality and a lack of one-on-one interaction.

One goal of a group mentoring situation that differs from individual mentoring is to encourage group members to help each other in addition to the assistance they receive from the mentor. This community approach to mentoring can prove beneficial to the protégés, as it creates a network of support and encouragement and opens further avenues for opportunity.

When establishing a group mentorship, it is important to be absolutely clear on objectives and expectations on all sides. As a group mentor, you will need a strong sense of commitment and an abundance of enthusiasm. You will also need negotiation and management skills—in any group, there will be disagreements, and you should be ready to smooth ruffled feathers at a moment's notice.

# Protégé Profits

The obvious benefit for the mentor in a group setting is the ability to develop multiple protégés simultaneously. There are also benefits for protégés participating in group mentoring. Many people do not feel comfortable working one-on-one with a superior, and would therefore thrive in a group setting where all the focus is not directed on them and their performance. A group format is also more flexible, less formal, and more social than single encounters.

Of course, there are problems that uniquely pertain to a group setting. With planning and strong leadership, you can overcome problems and direct a dynamic mentor group. Some of the potential difficulties include:

- A lack of candid feedback
- Uneven learning experience and frequent repetition
- Low accountability for the success of the group
- Dominance by a single personality

I personally would favor one on one mentoring over the group. The group scenario makes everyone feel the same, whether you want to believe it or not. So there really are limitations as to how far you can develop individual strengths in a group.

Sometimes the group scenario can be used to select the best prospects for further, one on one mentoring. In this fashion, you won't have to spend as much time figuring out if a person is right for mentoring. You had the chance to do so by taking on the personal commitment.

## Protégé Profits

Groups, in general, are limiting and it's why communists and socialists love them so much – because they are exclusive. They are exclusive of allowing a person to expand beyond a group when the group no longer shares the vision. Developing the individual responsibly allows them to live their personal vision when others have gotten lazy. Groups breed dependency. Your mentorship mission is to break dependencies, and breed creativity and life without responsible limits.

# Chapter 9
## Repeating The Process

When you have successfully trained a protégé and your mentorship ends, it is beneficial to keep your momentum going. You may want to give yourself a cooling-off period to reflect on the process before beginning again, but if the mentoring program was successful, you should continue to act as a mentor.

Do not forget that mentoring is a two-way street. You will learn as much from your protégés as they learn from you. By continuing to mentor, you will gain diversification, new life outlooks, and the satisfaction of having assisted several young people in launching their careers. This reflects positively on you, both professionally and personally.

When you are ready to find another protégé, you can simply return to the beginning of the selection process and start fresh. There are also additional options for finding a new protégé once you have completed a mentorship.

**Referrals from your protégés**

During the mentoring process, you and your protégé will have gotten to know each other well. You will be familiar with each other's likes and dislikes; your personal and professional goals; your personalities and preferences. This makes your former protégé an excellent resource for discovering new protégés to take on.

If you plan to continue mentoring, you should bring this issue to light at the dissolution of the mentor-protégé relationship.

# Protégé Profits

Let your protégé know that you will be looking for another newcomer to assist as you have assisted them, and ask him or her to keep an eye out for likely candidates. Even if your protégé continues working at your company, he will likely have different experiences and may move in slightly different circles.

College interns can also sometimes make good recommendations regarding other college students. Interaction between college students does not tend to be separated by grade level; rather, students are familiar with others who are majoring in the same subjects. A graduating senior college student may know of some promising juniors who would be ready to intern soon.

Referrals which you can act on with confidence will lessen your workload when it comes to taking on new protégés. You should still initiate a formal investigation and interview process with a potential protégé—but in the case of referrals, you will only need to perform the process once, and there is no pressure to decide between multiple qualified candidates.

## After-retirement mentoring

Mentoring after retirement can sometimes be more rewarding than mentoring during your career. At this point, you have likely gained a wealth of knowledge that will prove immensely beneficial to any protégé.

Retirement also allows you to involve yourself in mentoring on a full-time basis. With the restrictions of time and quality erased, you may find that you are able to truly make a difference in the direction of a protégé's career. Your protégé will be appreciative of the ability to spend more time working with you. You will also be more flexible in regards to meeting locations, as you can interact at any time.

Post-retirement boredom is practically a disease. It is easy to slip into complacency after retirement and allow the mind to become clouded and dull. A lack of direction and focus has led many retired professionals to a less than satisfying existence. Mentoring will allow you to continue performing the work you love, without the restrictions of your job responsibilities. It will also allow you to keep a finger on the pulse of your industry, and remain current with developments and rising stars—which could include your protégé.

I personally don't believe in retiring, because of the suggestion of not being valuable. You are valuable as long as you envision yourself as such. So I like to think of the transition from career person, to business owner, to full-time mentor as a growth experience, not a retirement experience. You are only too old if you think so. There is no such thing as being too old. Look around you. There are very old people doing wonderful things, while others just talk about being too old.

The seniors doing the wonderful things definitely do not sit around talking about how they are too old for creativity and change. Don't retire, just improve, and never believe you are too old.

# Protégé Profits

# Final thoughts

Mentoring is one of the oldest and most satisfying pursuits in the history of civilization. Knowledge passed on from person to person has always been perceived as the most valuable, and the most memorable. As a mentor, you are achieving the personal satisfaction of helping a young person succeed, as well as the recognition as a knowledgeable and generous expert in your field.

Here are some key thoughts to keep in mind as you begin your mentoring journey:

- Mentoring is not an arranged marriage, but a partnership involving an exchange of ideas. Both parties learn from one another.
- As a mentor, you are not a guru passing on wisdom; rather, you are a facilitator of knowledge. Present yourself as an open conduit instead of an unapproachable fount.
- In addition to skills and business behaviors, you will be passing on attitudes and capabilities to your protégé. Remember that your protégé will learn as much from what you do not say as from what you say. A positive attitude is imperative for a successful mentor.
- Do not limit the development of your protégé by your shared agenda. Remain open to new ideas that arise during the process, and encourage dialogue exchange and free-form thinking. Explore every possibility.
- Refrain from focusing on promotions and company advancement during the course of your mentoring program. Instead, become project-centric: make

# Protégé Profits

change and accomplishment more central to your objectives than outside recognition. In most cases, career advancement will be an automatic side effect of a successful mentorship for both you and your protégé.
- Think of your protégé as a mature child rather than a charity case. Focus on those activities and strategies that will help your protégés to help themselves, rather than attempting to hand them success. Your protégés should be able to succeed on their own merits without resting on your laurels. As a mentor, your task is to enable, rather than produce, success.

Careful selection and grooming of a protégé can lead to one of the most rewarding relationships of your life. The mutually beneficial aspects of the mentor-protégé relationship have far-reaching implications beyond the office or company. Above all, it is most important that both you and your protégé derive comfort and enjoyment from the relationship, and forge a connection that will last a lifetime.

In the end, your continuing development of protégés will bring you and ever growing stream of business relationships you can depend on because you know the person you are dealing with inside and out.

In fact, as a business owner, you are likely to find the person you want to run your company when you no longer want to do this. You will live your personal vision as a result. Your life will be fulfilled, and you will never feel too old to add value.

## Protégé Profits

Your protégé offers you wealth and fulfillment you likely never imagined. Don't pass this up in your life of making a radical difference for others.

> *"The unselfish effort to bring cheer to others will be the beginning of a happier life for ourselves".*
> ~Helen Keller~

# Protégé Profits

# Appendix
## How to Be a Professional Altruist

Mentoring has always been a noble pursuit. Those who volunteer their time in a mentor capacity are universally admired and respected. However, your altruistic intentions do not have to solely benefit your protégés or society as a whole. There are many ways to use protégés in your business or company that will help you as you are helping them.

Though some may balk at the idea, protégés can spell free labor for you. This is particularly applicable if you are a successful entrepreneur running your own business. Taking on protégés is immensely beneficial on both sides. A protégé who works directly with a business owner is able to view every aspect of what makes a successful business work.

This is the type of education you cannot buy through books or classes. Nothing is better than hands-on experience when it comes to real world working strategy. The protégé who is taken on by an entrepreneur has perhaps a greater advantage than those who work within a company: he will be equipped with the skills to start his own business and become successful in his own right.

Of course, protégés can be more useful to an entrepreneur than to a corporate employee as well. Absent the necessity of a formal, structured program, the mentor is free to introduce whatever skills and experience she deems necessary for the protégé's success. To an entrepreneur, protégés can provide the means to move a business forward while simultaneously helping young people off to a great start in the business world. They learn how to add value and get people real solutions they seek.

If you are a business owner and would like to make use of protégés to benefit both your business and your community, you can follow the same procedures to select and groom protégés throughout the life cycle of your company. However, you should follow a slightly different set of qualifications for your protégés. Entrepreneurs require greater drive and independence for success.

Some of the aspects a successful entrepreneurial protégé should possess include:

- Leadership qualities
- A healthy drive for success
- Realistic business expectations
- Developed work ethic
- Fresh ideas and a strong business premise
- Energy and passion
- Innovative tendencies
- Self-possession
- A positive attitude
- The ability to learn from mistakes
- Thick skin
- Resourcefulness
- "Out of the box" thinking
- Honesty and integrity
- Delegation ability
- Stress and time management skills
- Strong communication abilities
- Willingness to ask for help when needed

## Protégé Profits

- Creativity and flexibility
- Strong initiative
- The power of persuasion
- Knowledge of a chosen industry

Business owners who take on protégés have the ability to invest more time and effort in the mentoring process than their corporately employed counterparts. They are also able to realize greater benefits by employing protégés, as the knowledge and resources to start a business is powerful motivation to succeed.

You can become a professional altruist and create a business that thrives on helping young people develop their skills and qualifications. Your business will profit morally and financially through your use of protégés, and those who are assisted by your generosity will not hesitate to return the favor.

# Protégé Profits

# About The Author

Wayne Sharer is the bestselling author of the anthology, "The Art and Science of Success Volume 2." He has lived a lifetime of mentorship with exceptional skills in creating radical improvements everywhere he goes.

Wayne's life is that of pure determination and self-motivation, yet very selfless. Through his own determination, despite being from an extremely lower middle-class upbringing, attended one of the best Universities in the country at Tulane University in New Orleans, Louisiana.

He earned a Reserve Officers Training Corp scholarship in 1976 and went on to graduate from Tulane with a bachelor's degree in Biology. At graduation, he was commissioned an Ensign in the United States Navy. Owing only 4 years of service, he stayed on for 22 years, rising to the rank of Commander, and serving as a Commanding Officer of an E-2C Airborne Early Warning Hawkeye squadron. His squadron was one of the most successful of its time.

In the Navy he flew nearly 3,000 hours in the Hawkeye, flew on over 200 combat missions spanning from 1981 to 2002. He served on 6 different aircraft carriers, ran the operations of over 5,000 people on board the USS Kitty Hawk, the first carrier to launch combat missions in response to terrorists' attacks of September 11, 2001.

He considers his greatest accomplishments having been able to mentor thousands of young people and help them define their visions, and go onto success in life.

## Protégé Profits

After his fall from the Navy, he started over as an entrepreneur, mastering the art of generating leads and traffic using the internet. He then went back to his professional roots and began training new entrepreneurs in these very skills, and has created what amounts to a "university" of online lead generation called "Layered Traffic™" at his website **YourTrafficStarterBlog.com**.

His business now trains entrepreneurs and provides services to small businesses for getting them leads, and customers using the power of the internet.

His company is now taking a lead role in online reputation marking, and you can evaluate your company online through his free software at ZagatReputationRepair.com

He and his business partner also work to help companies and organizations that train and develop skills of what some called the underprivileged. In reality, they have the same privileges as you and I, and they are now serious about also developing personally.

Everything Wayne undertakes is about creating radical change in peoples' lives and helping them realize their personal vision.

Wayne now lives in Washington, DC, working completely virtually and from home. He's available for speaking and training events and can be reached at **wayne@thinkbigandgrow.com** or by using the contact forms on his websites, including **WayneSharer.com**.

# Protégé Profits

**Protégé Profits**

www.ingramcontent.com/pod-product-compliance
Lightning Source LLC
Chambersburg PA
CBHW061512180526
45171CB00001B/151